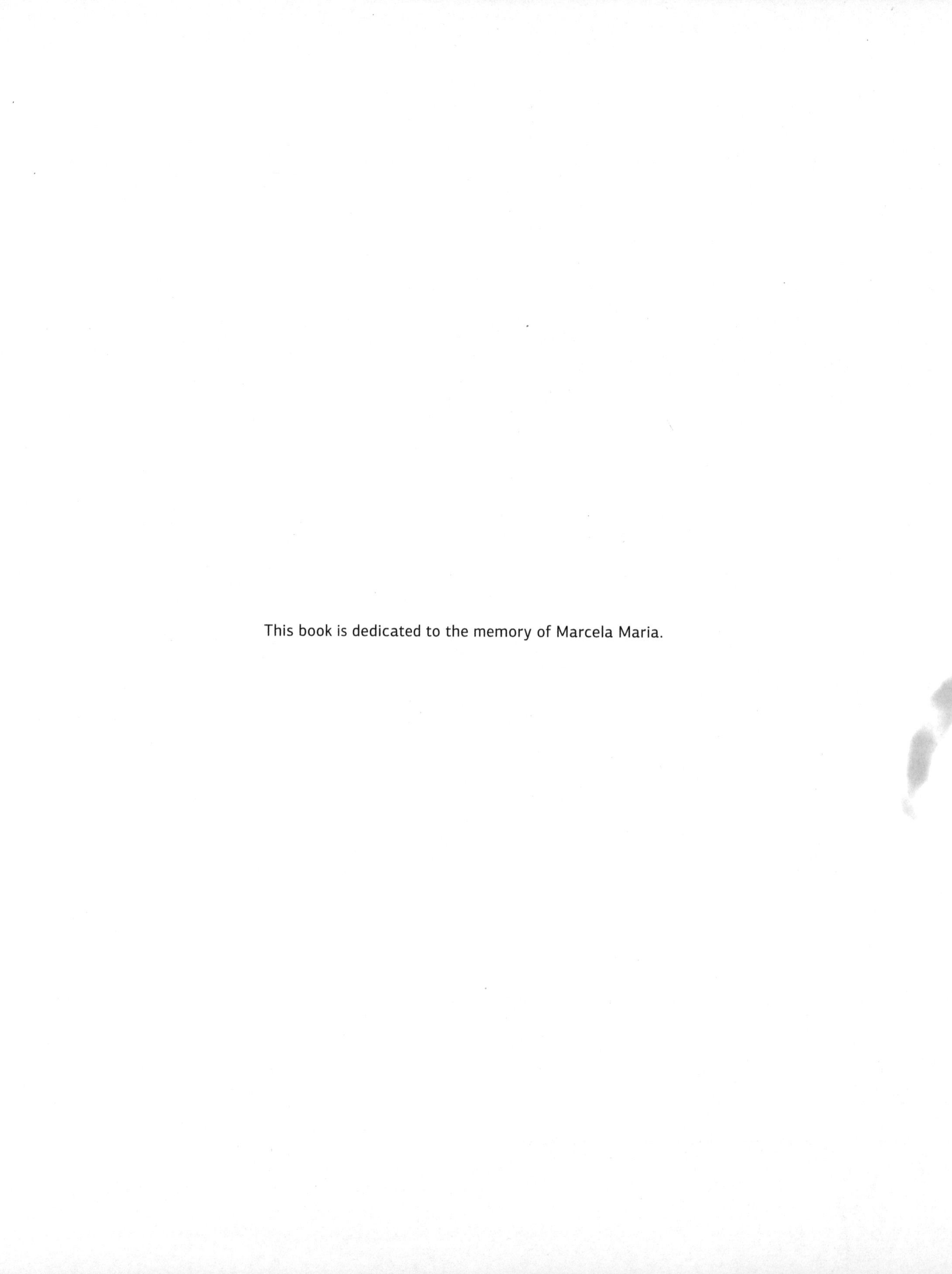

This book is dedicated to the memory of Marcela Maria.

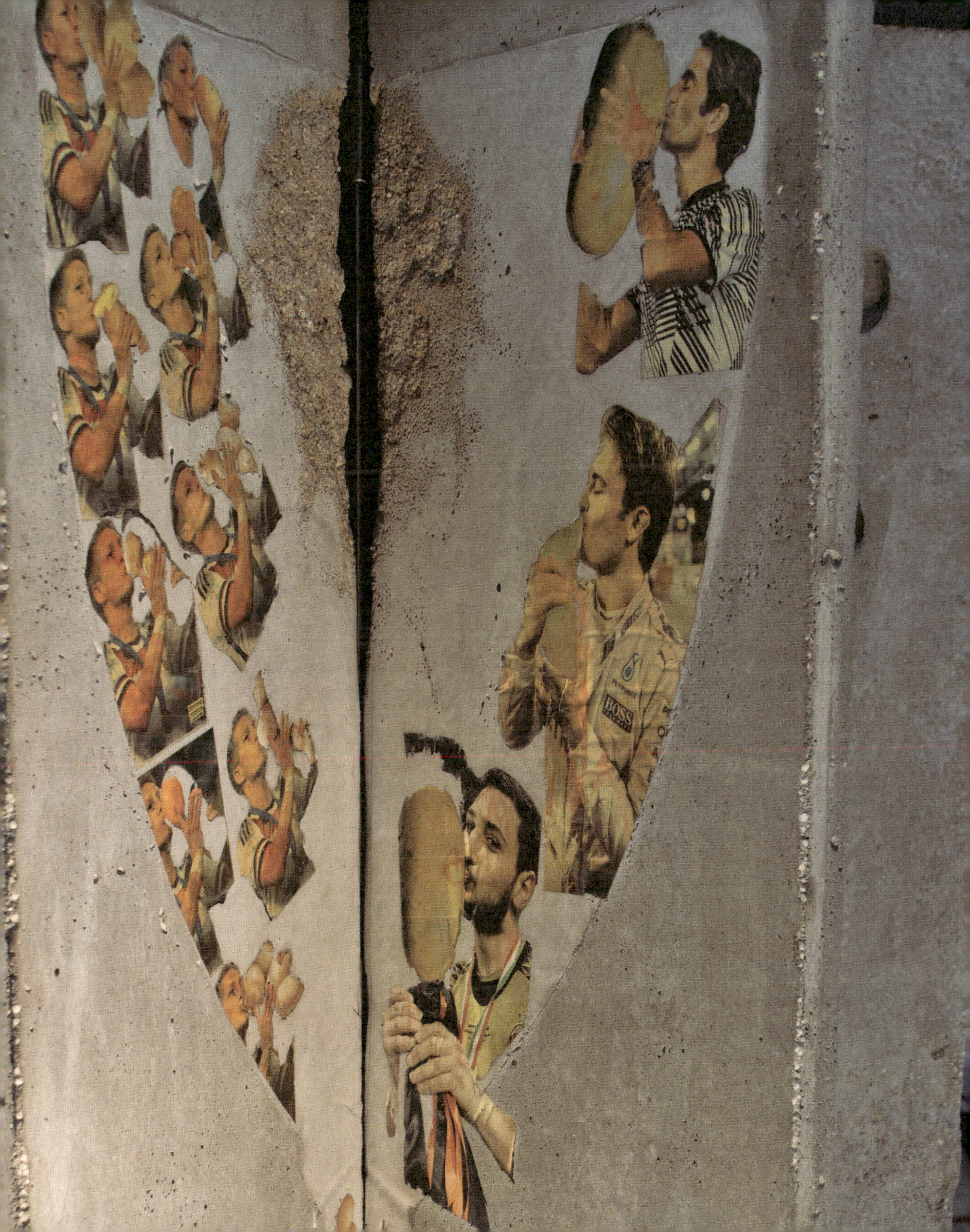
BOSS

MATHEUS ROCHA PITTA

AOS VENCEDORES AS BATATAS

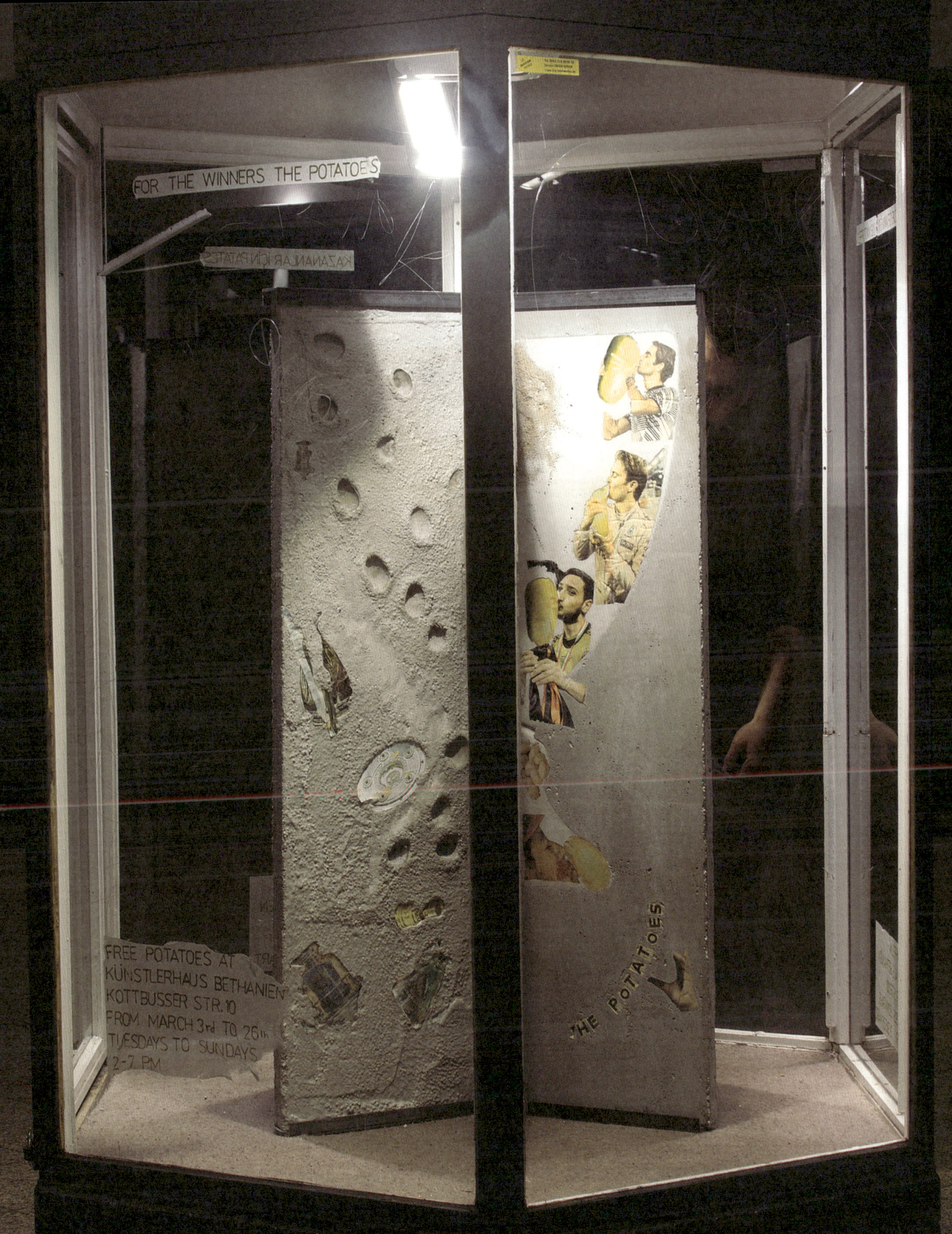
FOR THE WINNERS THE POTATOES
FREE POTATOES AT
KÜNSTLERHAUS BETHANIEN
KOTTBUSSER STR.10
FROM MARCH 3rd TO 26th
TUESDAYS TO SUNDAYS
12-7 PM
THE POTATOES

Preface

Column # 1 (potato podium)
metal structure, concrete, paper and removed potatoes
130 x 36 x 4 cm each, six concrete slabs
2016/2017
Gesundbrunnen U8 underground station

Promoting cultural diversity is the primary goal of KfW Stiftung. Together with Künstlerhaus Bethanien, we have set up an artist-in-residence programme that seeks to stimulate intercultural dialogue by providing artists from Africa, Asia, Latin America, and the Middle East with the opportunity to spend twelve months in Berlin. Besides encouraging artistic production and critical reflection, the programme facilitates encounters between professionals in arts and culture. Künstlerhaus Bethanien, with its infrastructure and international environment, offers a suitable setting for this purpose, allowing participants to try out new ideas, engage in debates and carry out projects.

Artists are often expected to show site-specific insights devoid of local colour while also producing universally intelligible works outside the global mainstream. Given this situation, how do the artists' origins impact the perception of their works of art? Our artist-in-residence programme does not present artists as representatives of a particular country or culture. Rather, it creates the opportunity to question the existing links between international networks on the one hand and to examine specific geographic and culturally defined places on the other, thus generating new ways of thinking, making and perceiving.

Die Stärkung kultureller Vielfalt ist ein besonderes Anliegen der KfW Stiftung. Mit dem Ziel, den interkulturellen Dialog voranzutreiben, realisieren wir in Kooperation mit dem Künstlerhaus Bethanien ein Atelierprogramm, das Künstlern aus Lateinamerika, Afrika und Asien einen zwölfmonatigen Aufenthalt in Berlin ermöglicht. Künstlerische Produktion und kritische Reflexion sollen ebenso gefördert werden wie der Austausch mit anderen Kunst- und Kulturschaffenden. Die Infrastruktur und das internationale Umfeld des Künstlerhauses bieten eine Plattform zu experimentieren, zu diskutieren und Projekte zu realisieren.

Welche Rolle spielt jedoch die Herkunft eines Künstlers für die Rezeption seines Werks, wenn einerseits ortsspezifische Authentizität ohne Lokalkolorit, andererseits universelle Lesbarkeit ohne globalen Mainstream erwartet wird? Unser Atelierprogramm teilt Künstlern nicht die Rolle von nationalen Repräsentanten zu. Vielmehr zeigt sich, dass internationale Vernetzung und die Auseinandersetzung mit bestimmten geografischen und kulturell geprägten Orten miteinander verknüpft sind und so neue Denk- und Sichtweisen entstehen.

Ulrich Schröder
Board KfW Stiftung

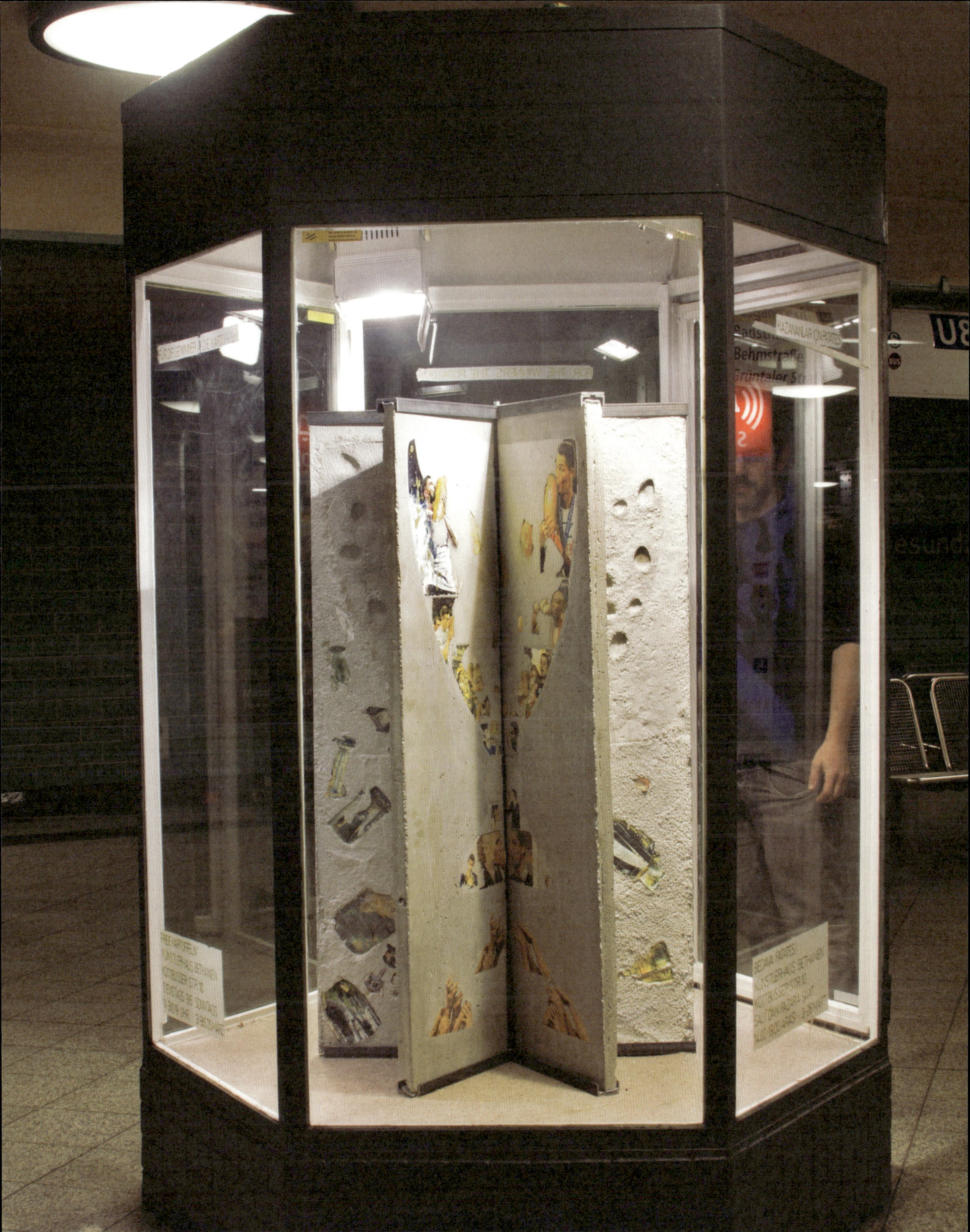
Behmstraße
U8

Contents

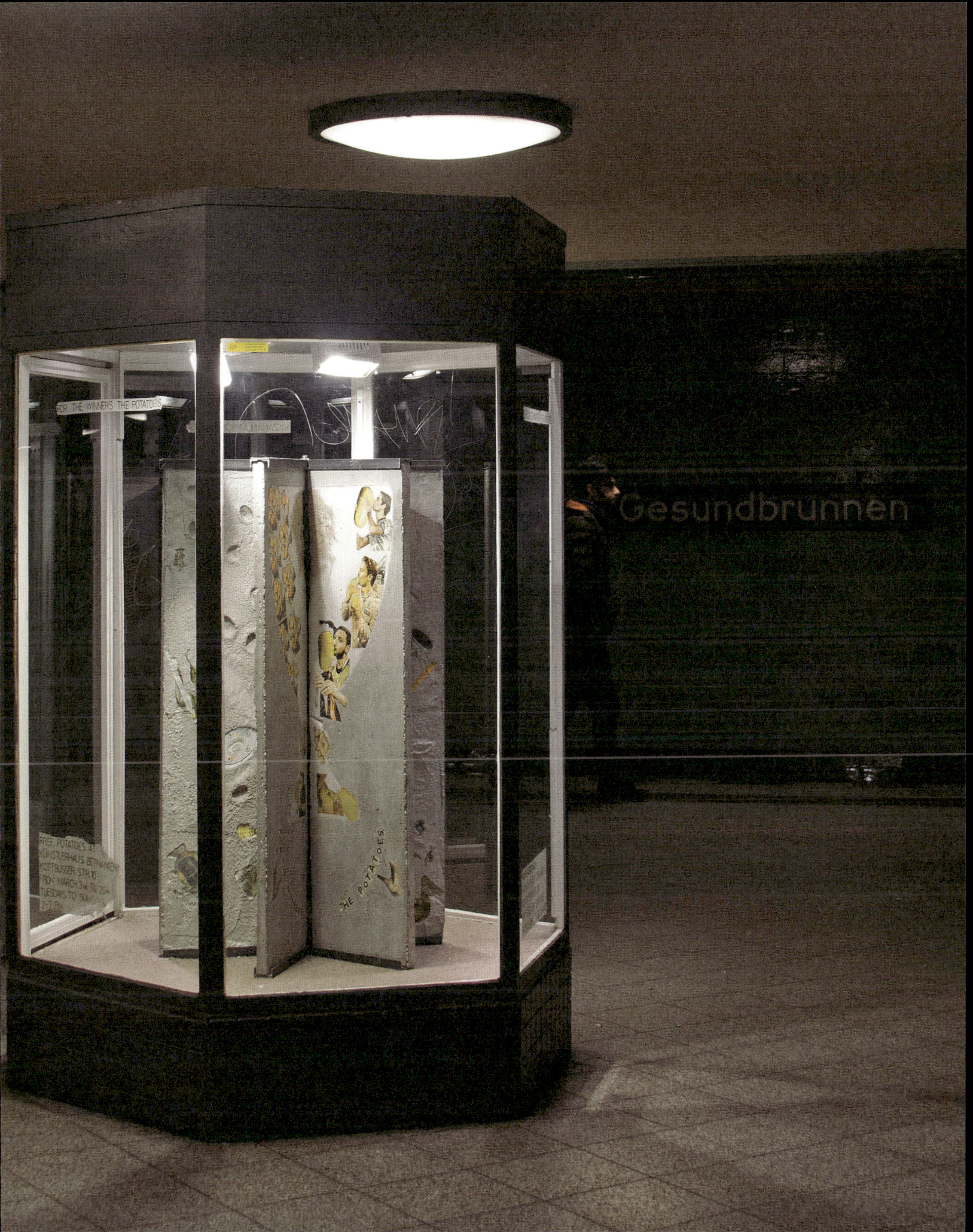

FOR THE WINNERS THE POTATOES
Gesundbrunnen

Victory begins in the mind: Potatoes for the winners

by Tobias Peper

"All emerged victorious, even if only one can be the winner" – an entire generation in Germany grew up with this well-intentioned, chanted contradiction. The words appeared in the closing song of the *Mini Playback Show*, a hugely successful forerunner of the modern day casting show, broadcast on the country's largest private TV channel from 1990 to 1998. Children competed against each other with the ambition of imitating their musical heroes on stage as convincingly as possible, but instead of singing live they lip-synched to pre-recorded songs. The winner received a big trophy and the "other winners" smaller trophies or consolation prizes. The show provided the feelgood soundtrack for the treaty signed in 1990 between the Federal Republic of Germany and the German Democratic Republic, which established the social market economy as the economic system and foundation for the reunification of the two countries.[1] Millions of children hummed the song and learned that we are all in competition with each other, but nobody is left out in the end.

As the Cold War era gradually came to a close, the liberalisation and globalisation of markets prevailed throughout the Western world in the following decade,

1 In 2007, the European Union agreed on this guiding model in the Treaty of Lisbon, and at the 2009 World Economic Forum in Davos Angela Merkel argued that as a lesson from the financial crisis this economic system was to be applied as the primary international principle.

Der Sieg beginnt im Kopf: Kartoffeln für die Gewinner

von Tobias Peper

„Alle waren Sieger, auch wenn einer nur gewinnen kann" – eine ganze Generation in Deutschland wuchs mit diesem wohlwollend gemeinten, gesungenen Widerspruch auf. Die Zeile entstammt dem Schlusslied der *Mini Playback Show*, einer von 1990 bis 1998 sehr erfolgreichen frühen Form der Castingshow auf dem größten Privatsender des Landes. Kinder traten mit dem Ziel gegeneinander an, ihren musikalischen Vorbildern möglichst authentisch auf der Bühne nachzueifern, wobei anstelle von Live-Gesang eine Playback-Spur zum Einsatz kam. Die Gewinner erhielten einen großen Pokal und die „anderen Sieger" etwas kleinere Trophäen sowie Trostpreise. Die Sendung lieferte den Wohlfühl-Soundtrack zu dem zwischen der Bundesrepublik und DDR unterzeichneten Staatsvertrag von 1990, in dem die soziale Marktwirtschaft als Wirtschaftsordnung und Grundlage der Wiedervereinigung beider Länder festgelegt wurde.[1] Millionen von Kindern summten den Hit mit und lernten, dass wir zwar alle miteinander im Wettbewerb stehen, aber am Ende niemand vergessen wird.

Mit dem Ausklingen der Ära des Kalten Krieges setzten sich im folgenden Jahrzehnt in der westlichen Welt jedoch zunehmend die Liberalisierung und Globalisierung

1 Auch die Europäische Union hat sich im Vertrag von Lissabon 2007 auf dieses Leitbild geeinigt und 2009 propagierte Angela Merkel auf dem Weltwirtschaftsgipfel in Davos, dass man als Lehre aus der Finanzkrise diese Wirtschaftsform als international grundlegendes Prinzip anwenden sollte.

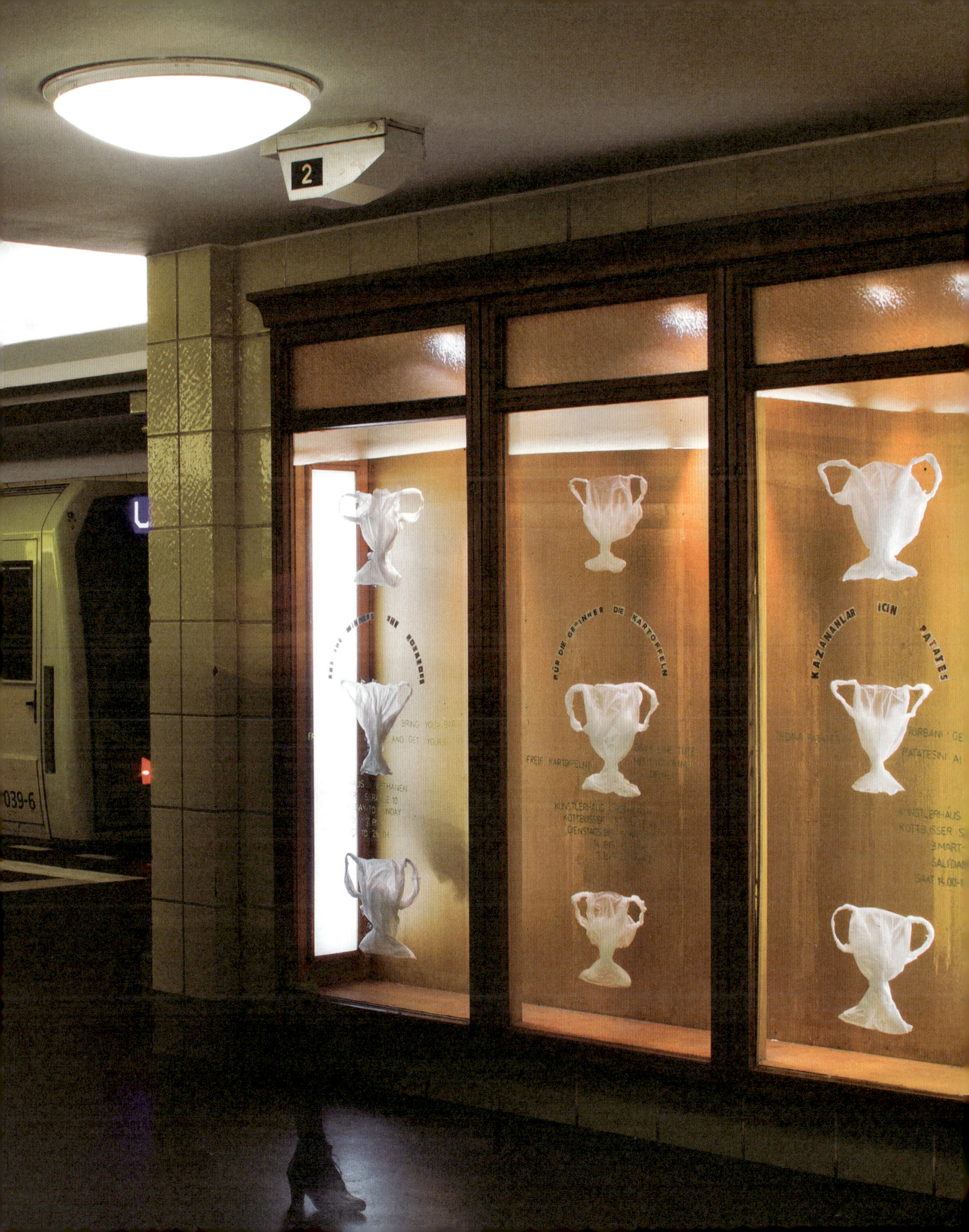
2
BRING YOUR BAG
AND GET YOURS
FÜR DIE GEWINNER DIE KARTOFFELN
KAZANANLAR İÇİN PATATES

giving little consideration to redistributive justice. In Germany, just before the new millennium, the children's song about prosperity for everyone died away; instead loud and violent arguments erupted over alleged social spongers, while the Agenda 2010 (a major programme of reforms) was prepared behind the scenes.

Today, our solidarity as a community, which was once the foundation of our peaceful coexistence, seems to have become a crisis-ridden pile of rubble. The fear of terrorism as well as banking and refugee crises that are being put forward have changed the international rhetoric. The populism of our time exploits the feeling of being left behind, a feeling haunting many people, and preaches the opposite of social, cultural and economic participation by pushing national ambitions. Instead of seeking social equity and unity, nowadays we once again live by the maxim: "The winner takes it all, the loser standing small." In his most recent work, developed during a one-year stay in Germany, the Brazilian artist Matheus Rocha Pitta addresses this shift and its consequences for our sense of community.

The multi-part installation *For the winners the potatoes* (2017), his final project created as grant holder of KfW Stiftung in Berlin at the international cultural centre Künstlerhaus Bethanien and in two of the city's underground stations, deconstructs the principle of victory and the hierarchy of winners and losers in a humorous way and unravels a complex web of historical references which goes back as far as ancient Greece and raises fundamental questions about the status of the community. The title is taken from a key passage of the novel *Quincas Borba* (1891) written by Joaquim Maria Machado de Assis. The novel is still popular in Brazil today, but is little known anywhere else in the world, although it has been translated into English and German.[2] The plot revolves around the character of Rubião, who acquires

2 Assis, Machado de: *Quincas Borba*. Frankfurt am Main: Suhrkamp, 1982.
Assis, Machado de: *Philosopher or Dog?* New York City: Farrar, Straus and Giroux, 1992.

Trophy gallery
plastic bags, paper and tape
variable dimensions
2016/2017
Hermannplatz U8 underground station

der Märkte durch, die wenig Rücksicht auf eine ausgleichende Solidarität nahmen. Auch in Deutschland verstummte kurz vor der Jahrtausendwende das kindliche Lied vom Wohlstand für alle, stattdessen stritt man sich laut und heftig über vermeintliche Sozialschmarotzer, während die Agenda 2010 hinter den Kulissen vorbereitet wurde.

Heute erscheint die Verbundenheit als Gemeinschaft, die einst die Grundlage unseres Zusammenlebens war, wie ein krisengeschüttelter Scherbenhaufen vor uns zu liegen. Die postulierte Angst vor Terrorismus, Banken- und Flüchtlingskrisen haben die internationale Rhetorik verändert. Der Populismus unserer Zeit macht sich das Gefühl des Abgehängtseins, das viele Menschen verfolgt, zunutze und propagiert mit nationalen Bestrebungen das Gegenteil von sozialer, kultureller und wirtschaftlicher Partizipation. Anstatt nach Ausgleich und Einheit zu suchen, heißt das Prinzip heute wieder „The winner takes it all, the loser standing small." Der brasilianische Künstler Matheus Rocha Pitta verhandelt in seiner jüngsten Arbeit, die während eines einjährigen Aufenthalts in Deutschland entstanden ist, eben jene Verschiebung und deren Konsequenz für unser Miteinander.

Die mehrteilige Installation *For the winners the potatoes* (2017), die als Abschluss seines Stipendiums der KfW Stiftung im Künstlerhaus Bethanien in Berlin und an zwei U-Bahnhöfen der Stadt entstand, dekonstruiert das Prinzip des Siegens, die Hierarchie von Gewinner und Verlierer auf humorvolle Art und Weise und entspinnt ein vielgliedriges historisches Referenzgeflecht, das bis in die griechische Antike zurückreicht und grundlegende Fragen nach dem Status der Gemeinschaft stellt. Der Titel der Arbeit entstammt einer Schlüsselstelle des Romans *Quincas Borba* (1891) von Joaquim Maria

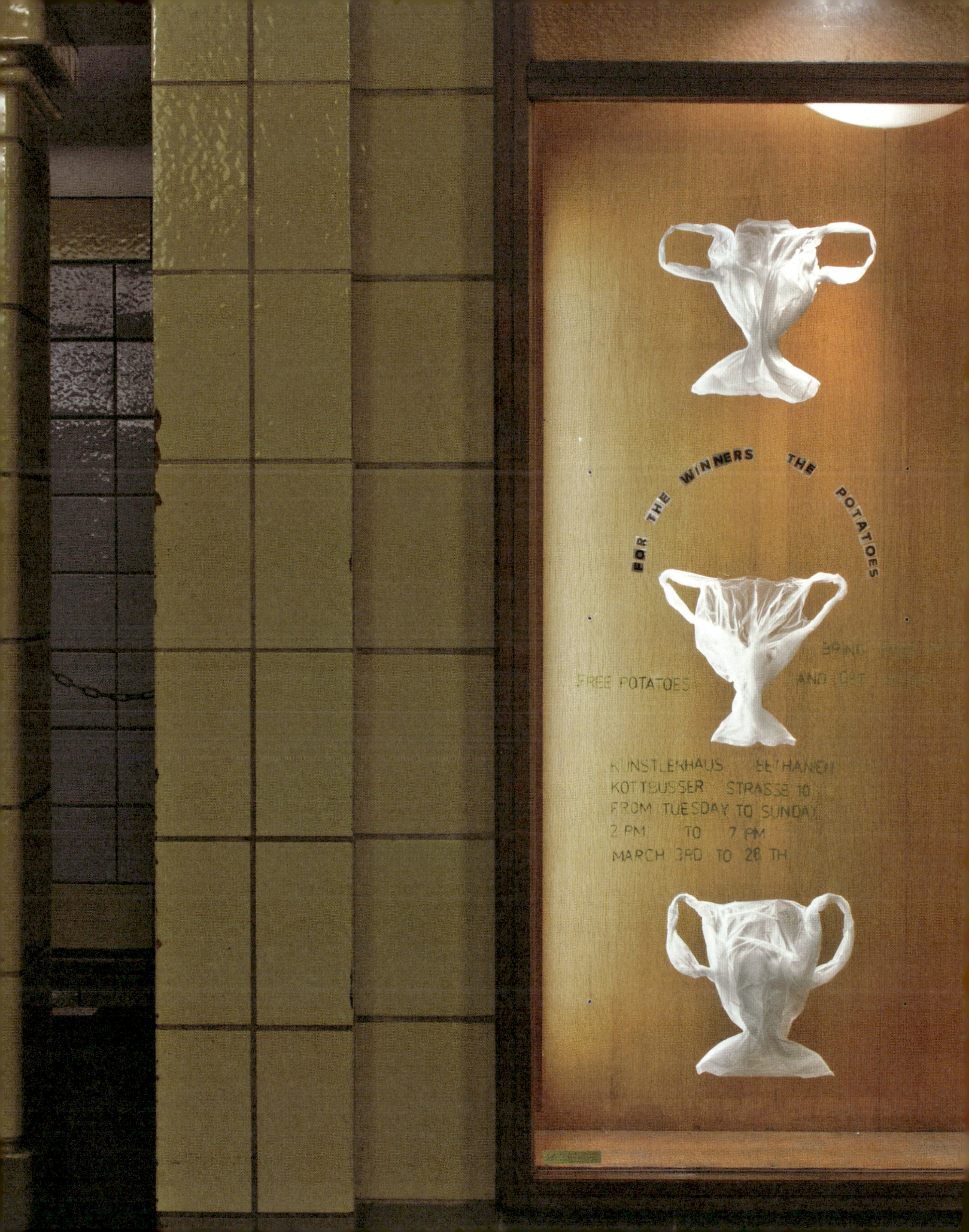
FOR THE WINNERS THE POTATOES
FREE POTATOES
BRING
AND GET
KÜNSTLERHAUS BETHANIEN
KOTTBUSSER STRASSE 10
FROM TUESDAY TO SUNDAY
2 PM TO 7 PM
MARCH 3RD TO 28 TH

a fortune as the sole heir of his teacher, the philosopher Quincas Borba. Shortly before his death, Borba tells his student a parable which presents the core of his own "humanitismo" theory. Two starving communities are faced with the prospect of a potato field. However, it can only feed one of the two communities. A peaceful agreement and a fair division of the harvest would thus inevitably result in the downfall of both societies. In this case, peace represents destruction and war survival. With this story Quincas Borba explains the cheers, anthems, public ceremonies and other joys of victory that are associated with any warlike action and determine its nature. He remarks that human beings only ever celebrate what they regard as pleasant and profitable. Borba concludes his reflections by phrasing the contrast: "Hatred or sympathy for the vanquished. Potatoes for the winners." His apprentice Rubião believes he has understood the core of the story: when he receives his inheritance, he imagines he has come into possession of the metaphorical potatoes. He heads to a big city where he intends to reap the fruits of his supposed destiny as a winner. He falls in love with a young woman whose actual lover takes advantage of the situation and relieves Rubião of his money through deceit. Heartbroken, impoverished and driven mad by the blows of fate incomprehensible to him, Rubião dies in the streets of Rio de Janeiro. His last words are: "For the winner the potatoes".

In his novel, Machado de Assis examines the theory of Social Darwinism popular in his day with irony and pessimism and illustrates the inhuman effects that arise if nothing but the principle of the survival of the fittest is applied to our life in society. Moreover, he depicts the destructive power that unfolds when holding on to any supposedly universal truth – for his enlightened hero Rubião is doomed to death.

As the key feature of *For the winners the potatoes* Rocha Pitta invents a three-dimensional equivalent of the novel's meaningful parable. Seven trophies made of

Machado de Assis. Das Werk wird in Brasilien bis heute viel rezipiert, ist im Rest der Welt jedoch kaum bekannt, gleichwohl eine englische und deutsche Übersetzung vorliegen.[2] Die Handlung kreist um die Figur Rubião, der als Alleinerbe seines Lehrers, dem Philosophen Quincas Borba, Reichtum erlangt. Kurz vor seinem Tod erzählt Borba seinem Schüler eine Parabel, die den Kern der von ihm erdachten Lehre „Humanitismo" enthält. Darin sind zwei hungernde Volksgruppen mit der Aussicht auf ein Kartoffelfeld konfrontiert. Das Feld kann jedoch nur eine der beiden ernähren, sodass eine friedliche Einigung und ein Aufteilen der Ernte zum unweigerlichen Untergang beider Gesellschaften führen würde. Friede bedeutet in diesem Fall Zerstörung und Krieg das Fortbestehen. Quincas Borba erklärt mit dieser Erzählung den Jubel, die Hymnen, öffentliche Ehrungen und andere Freuden des Sieges, die mit jeder kriegsähnlichen Handlung verbunden seien und ihr Wesen bestimmen. Er fügt hinzu, dass der Mensch stets nur das ihm Angenehme und Vorteilhafte feiere. Borba endet seine Ausführungen mit der Gegenüberstellung: „Hass oder Mitgefühl für die Besiegten. Kartoffeln für die Sieger". Sein Lehrling Rubião meint den Kern der Erzählung begriffen zu haben, als er sich mit dem erhaltenen Erbe im Besitz der metaphorischen Kartoffeln wähnt. Er macht sich auf in die Großstadt, wo er die Früchte seiner vermeintlichen Bestimmung als Sieger zu ernten gedenkt. Er verliebt sich in eine junge Frau, deren eigentlicher Liebhaber jedoch diese Situation ausnutzt und Rubião durch Betrug um sein Geld bringt. Mit gebrochenem Herzen, verarmt und über die ihm unbegreiflichen Schicksalsschläge verrückt geworden stirbt Rubião in den Straßen Rio de Janeiros. Seine letzten Worte sind: „Für den Sieger die Kartoffeln".

Mit Ironie und Pessimismus verhandelt Machado de Assis in seinem Roman den zu seiner Zeit populären Sozialdarwinismus und vergegenwärtigt die unmenschlichen

2 Assis, Machado de: *Quincas Borba*. Frankfurt am Main: Suhrkamp, 1982.
Assis, Machado de: *Philosopher or Dog?* New York City: Farrar, Straus and Giroux, 1992.

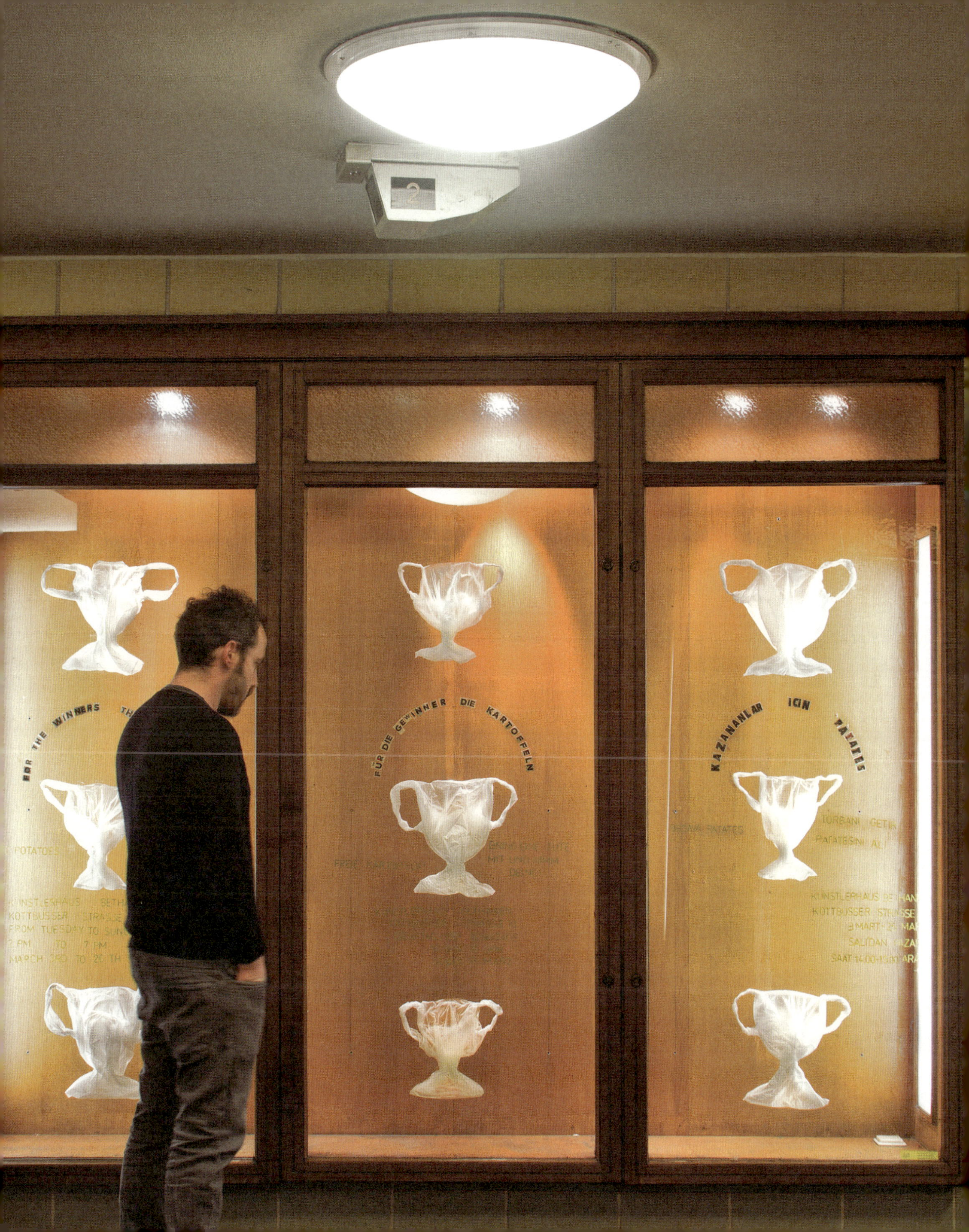
FÜR DIE GEWINNER DIE KARTOFFELN
KAZANANLAR İÇİN PATATES

concrete are presented in a chillingly illuminated showroom on a long, low glass table supported by pale bricks. The coarse casts are taken from standard vases which were filled with plastic bags in order to be able to release the hardened mass again. The bags are an integral part of the objects and sometimes provide handles. In an oval shape around the trophy altar, the artist has arranged plastic bags filled with potatoes whose handles are connected with each other like a chain. Words written on the wall invite the public to help itself to the offered gifts: "These potatoes are for you, take them freely but use your own bag."

Before entering the room, the visitor is greeted by a large and rectangular concrete slab in which letters and pictures from newspapers have been cast. Rocha Pitta used a production method from Brazil which he discovered at a cemetery in Belo Horizonte. Those who can't afford a tombstone for their deceased can make one for themselves using concrete. The moulds used for this purpose have no base and are therefore lined with newspaper to create a barrier for the liquid cement mixture at the bottom. When the finished slab is removed, bits and pieces of newspaper remain on the back. It is thus fitting that the title of the work *Estela #19 (For the winners the potatoes)* implicitly carries a reference to death, since a stele is a tombstone as well as a boundary stone, which separates the cult site with the trophies from the remaining rooms at Künstlerhaus Bethanien. The upper half of the slab announces "AOS VENCEDORES AS BATATAS", the title of the work in Portuguese. Below, pictures of trophies are arranged upside down in a semi-circle open towards the floor. They point to the lower half of the slab where a variety of newspaper clippings showing jubilant athletes are assembled in a triangle. Instead of holding their trophies, they are clutching, throwing or hugging potatoes. In the lower third, the pyramid of winners is rhythmically complemented by another semi-circle open towards the floor formed by potato marks in the concrete.

Auswirkungen, wenn einzig das Prinzip des Stärkeren auf das Miteinander angewendet wird. Darüber hinaus schildert er die destruktive Kraft, die mit jedem Festhalten an einer vermeintlich universellen Wahrheit einhergeht, indem Machado de Assis seinen erleuchteten Protagonisten Rubião dem Untergang weiht.

Als zentralen Moment von *For the winners the potatoes* inszeniert Rocha Pitta die plastische Entsprechung zur sinnstiftenden Parabel des Romans. Auf einem langen niedrigen Glastisch, der von hellen Bausteinen getragen wird, stehen sieben aus Beton gegossene Pokale in einem kalt ausgeleuchtetem Ausstellungsraum. Die groben Abgüsse sind aus handelsüblichen Vasen genommen, die mit Plastiktüten befüllt wurden, um die gehärtete Masse wieder auslösen zu können. Die Tüten sind Bestandteil der Objekte und formen mitunter die Henkel. In ovaler Formation um den Trophäenaltar hat der Künstler mit Kartoffeln gefüllte Plastiktüten arrangiert, deren Griffe wie in einer Kettenformation miteinander verbunden sind. Ein Schriftzug an der Wand fordert das Publikum zur Mitnahme der dargebotenen Gaben auf: „These potatoes are for you, take them freely but use your own bag."

Vor dem Betreten des Raums wird man von einer großen, rechteckigen Betontafel begrüßt, in die Buchstaben und Bildausschnitte aus Zeitungen gegossen sind. Das Herstellungsverfahren hat Rocha Pitta aus Brasilien übernommen, wo er auf einem Friedhof in Belo Horizonte darauf stieß. Wer sich keinen Grabstein für seine Toten leisten kann, produziert diesen selbst aus Beton. Die dafür verwendeten Gussformen haben keinen Boden und werden deswegen mit Zeitungspapier ausgelegt, um das flüssige Zementgemisch vom Grund abzugrenzen. Beim Entnehmen der fertigen Platte bleiben dabei Teile der Zeitungen auf der Rückseite haften. Passenderweise schwingt im Titel der Arbeit *Estela #19 (For the winners the potatoes)* auch die Referenz an den Tod mit, bezeichnet doch eine Stele einen Grabstein sowie einen Grenzstein, der im Künstlerhaus Bethanien

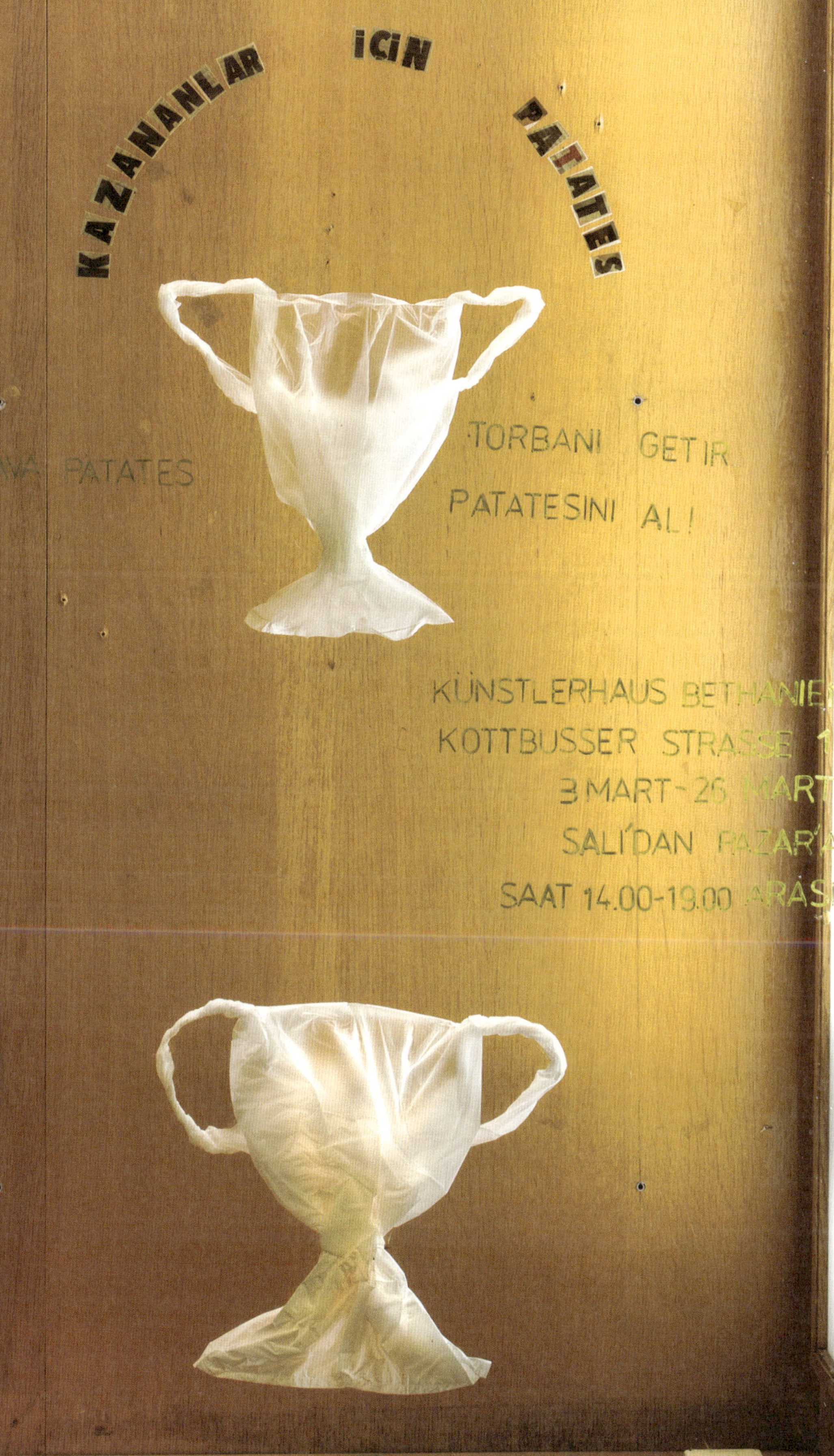
KAZANANLAR İÇİN PATATES
DAVA PATATES
TORBANI GETİR
PATATESİNİ AL!
KÜNSTLERHAUS BETHANIE
KOTTBUSSER STRASSE 10
3 MART - 26 MART
SALI'DAN PAZAR'A
SAAT 14.00-19.00 ARASI

A sign on the wall opposite the slab announces that the exhibition continues in two underground stations of the U8 line. In the station Gesundbrunnen, located in the middle of Berlin's Wedding borough, Rocha Pitta has radially arranged six concrete slabs of the same design in a hexagonal showcase. On the front and back visible to the viewer, one half of a trophy, which forms a whole with its corresponding neighbour – and from a distance even with the one after the next – is presented as a picture within the picture. Sometimes disembodied arms reach for the illustrated trophies. In this case, the hands belong to the German Chancellor Merkel exhibiting her typical gesture termed the Merkel "diamond". For his composition on the slabs, Rocha Pitta draws on the same visual devices as for his installation at Künstlerhaus Bethanien. He has clearly chosen a humorous approach for the public space. Some of the newspaper clippings show prominent athletes such as Cristiano Ronaldo, who are depicted caressing oversized potatoes instead of the cup they just won. At the foot of the trophies made of pictures and giving structure to the slabs, the clippings with the "real" trophies replaced by images of potatoes are exposed as if they had been carelessly dropped there. The glass plates of the showcase contain an advertisement in German, English and Turkish, stating that the potatoes can be collected free of charge at Künstlerhaus Bethanien during opening hours.[3] The title *Column # 1 (potato podium)* includes a tongue-in-cheek reference to the ancient world. The showcase is raised to the status of a column with deliberate pomposity, and the work displayed in it is declared to be a potato podium. Here, podium connotes both the place where winners are awarded their prizes as well as the place where people debate and exchange ideas.

In the underground station Hermannplatz in the borough of Neukölln, Rocha Pitta uses a showcase built into the wall. Under the title *Trophy gallery*, three trophies folded out of plastic bags are glued to each of the

3 Entry to the exhibition space is also free.

die kultische Stätte mit den Trophäen von den übrigen Räumen trennt. Die obere Hälfte der Tafel ist mit dem Titel gebenden, portugiesischen Zitat „AOS VENCEDORES AS BATATAS" überschrieben. Darunter sind in einem nach unten geöffnetem Halbkreis Abbildungen von Pokalen kopfüber angeordnet und weisen auf die untere Tafelhälfte, auf der im dreieckigen Aufbau verschiedene aus Zeitungen ausgeschnittene Sportlerinnen und Sportlern in Jubelpose versammelt sind. Anstelle ihrer Trophäen halten, werfen oder umarmen sie Kartoffeln. Die Siegerpyramide wird im unteren Drittel durch einen weiteren nach unten geöffneten Halbkreis von Abdrücken von Kartoffeln im Beton rhythmisiert.

An der Wand gegenüber der Tafel ist der Hinweis zu lesen, dass sich die Ausstellung an zwei Haltestellen der Linie U8 fortsetzt. Inmitten des Stadtteils Wedding im U-Bahnhof Gesundbrunnen hat Rocha Pitta in einem sechseckigen Schaukasten sechs Betonplatten gleicher Machart in radialer Anordnung installiert. Auf jeder sichtbaren Vorder- und Rückseite ist je ein halber Pokal als Bild im Bild inszeniert, der mit seinem entsprechendem Nachbarn ein Ganzes bildet – aus der Ferne auch mit der übernächsten Tafel. Bisweilen greifen körperlose Arme nach den illustrierten Trophäen, wobei es sich in einem Fall um die Hände von Bundeskanzlerin Merkel in typischer Rautenhaltung handelt. Für die Komposition auf den Platten greift Rocha Pitta auf dieselben Bildmittel zurück wie bei der Installation im Künstlerhaus Bethanien, wobei ein deutlich humorvoller Ansatz für den öffentlichen Raum gewählt wurde. So zeigen die Zeitungsausschnitte mitunter prominente Sportler wie Cristiano Ronaldo, die statt ihres soeben gewonnenen Pokals im Verhältnis überdimensionierte Kartoffeln liebkosen. Zu Füßen der aus Bildern geformten, die Tafeln strukturierenden Trophäen befinden sich wie achtlos fallen gelassen die Bildausschnitte der „echten" Pokale, welche durch die Abbildungen der Erdäpfel ersetzt wurden. An den Glasscheiben der Vitrine wirbt Rocha Pitta in deutscher, englischer und türkischer Sprache für die gratis Kartoffeln, die zu den Öffnungszeiten im

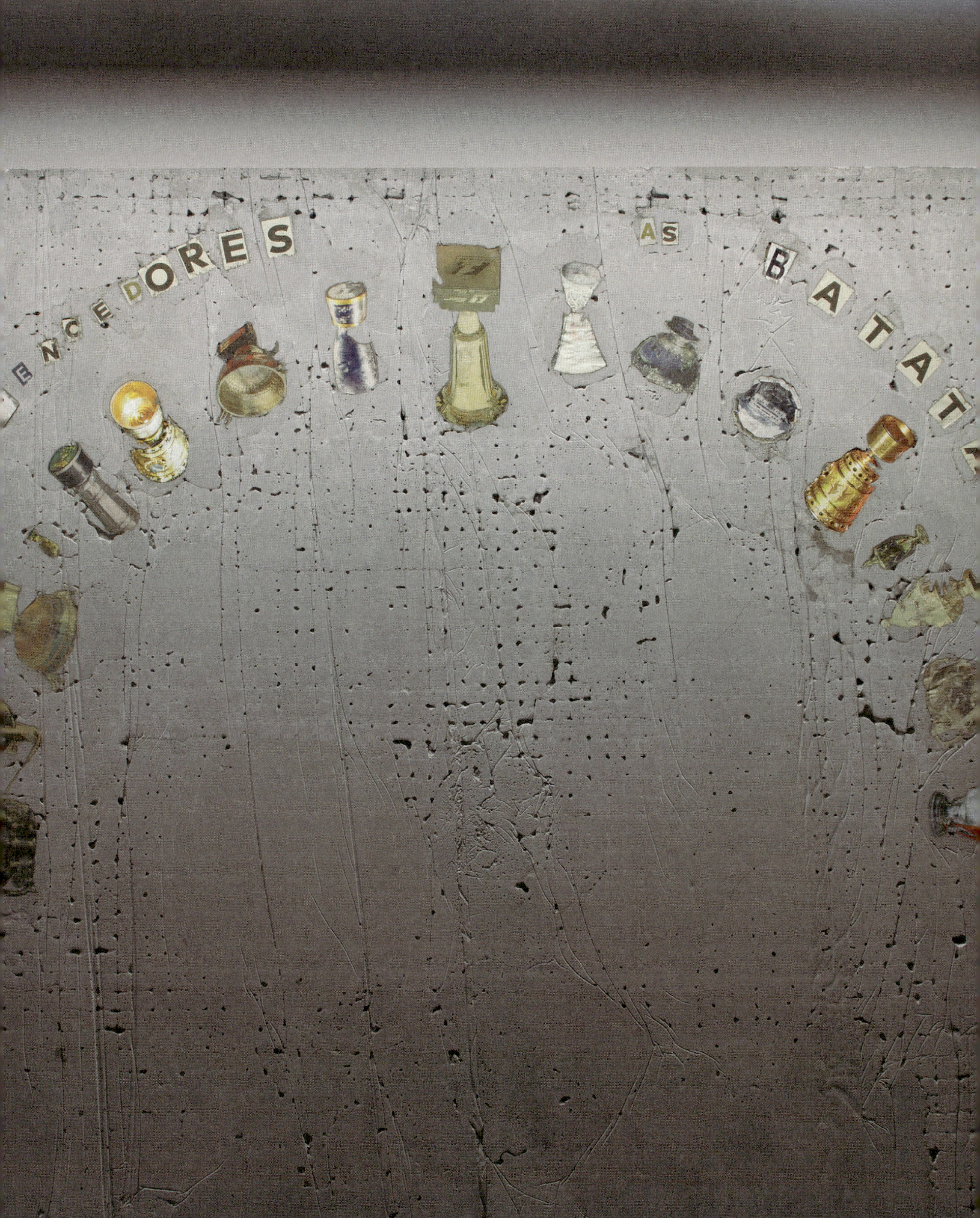
ENCEDORES
AS
BATAT

three glass plates. The title is written in German, Turkish and English in the form of an arch over the trophies in the middle. Again the letters have been cut out from newspapers, and in the three windows a trilingual sign refers to the free potatoes at Künstlerhaus Bethanien, located two underground stations away. From both underground stations you can reach the exhibition venue at Kottbusser Tor directly with the U8 line, without having to change trains. The transport junction is situated close to the geographical centre of the city in Alexandrinenstraße. In fact, the surrounding neighbourhood is known across the nation for its extreme social opposites. Rocha Pitta lived here during his one-year stay in Germany, and it is here that he bids farewell with a gesture of participation and exchange.

By expanding the exhibition into the public space, Rocha Pitta does not perform a classical intervention in the sense of interfering with existing conditions. He makes use of the given infrastructure, which already provides showcases in the underground stations, in order to issue an invitation to the city's residents via these means. It is not merely an advertisement for the exhibition, but a serious call for participation. This is confirmed by the fact that the leftover potatoes at the end of each day are delivered to the charity association Berliner Tafel, and thus benefit people in need. In addition, the public venues offer a surprising and bizarre moment outside everyday life for those passing by or waiting, as could easily be observed while the exhibition was on.

Rocha Pitta's installation in the city's inside and outside space can be interpreted on a more abstract level as an intervening gesture that captures and brings together several systems. First of all, he encroaches on the arena of international top-class sport in his concrete slabs. In his essay *The Sporting Spirit*, published in 1945, George Orwell identifies competitive sport as an outgrowth of aggressive nationalism, which in turn adds fuel to it.[4]

4 Cf. www.orwell.ru/library/articles/spirit/english/e_spirit (accessed 02.03.2017)

Stele # 19 (For the winners the potatoes)
concrete, paper and removed potatoes
180 x 90 x 4 cm
2016

Künstlerhaus Bethanien abgeholt werden können.[3] Der Titel *Column # 1 (potato podium)* beinhaltet einen augenzwinkernden Verweis auf die Antike. Bewusst großspurig wird die Vitrine zur Säule erhoben und die in ihr präsentierte Arbeit zum Kartoffelpodium erklärt, wobei das Podium sowohl als Ort der Siegerehrung als auch der Debatte und des Austauschs zu verstehen ist.

An der Haltestelle Hermannplatz in Neukölln hat Rocha Pitta einen in die Wand eingelassenen Schaukasten gestaltet. Unter dem Titel *Trophy gallery* sind an jede der drei Scheiben je drei aus Plastiktüten gefaltete Pokale geklebt, wobei die mittleren bogenförmig mit dem Ausstellungstitel auf deutsch, türkisch und englisch überschrieben sind. Die Buchstaben sind wieder aus Zeitungen ausgeschnitten. In den drei Fenstern findet sich erneut der dreisprachige Hinweis auf die kostenlosen Kartoffeln im zwei Stationen entfernten Künstlerhaus Bethanien. Von beiden Haltestellen ist der Ausstellungsort am Kottbusser Tor ohne Umstieg mit der Linie U8 zu erreichen. Der Verkehrsknotenpunkt liegt unweit des geographischen Zentrums der Stadt in der Alexandrinenstraße und seine Umgebung ist aufgrund extremer sozialer Gegensätze republikweit bekannt. Hier wohnte Rocha Pitta das Jahr über in Deutschland und hier begeht er seinen Abschied mit einer Geste der Teilhabe und des Austauschs.

Mit den Erweiterungen der Ausstellung in den öffentlichen Raum vollzieht Rocha Pitta keine klassische Intervention im Sinne eines Eingriffs in bestehende Zusammenhänge. Vielmehr nutzt er die gegebene Infrastruktur der vorhandenen Schaukästen in den U-Bahnhöfen, um mit ihrer Hilfe eine Einladung an die Bewohnerinnen und

3 Auch der Eintritt in die Ausstellungsräume ist kostenlos.

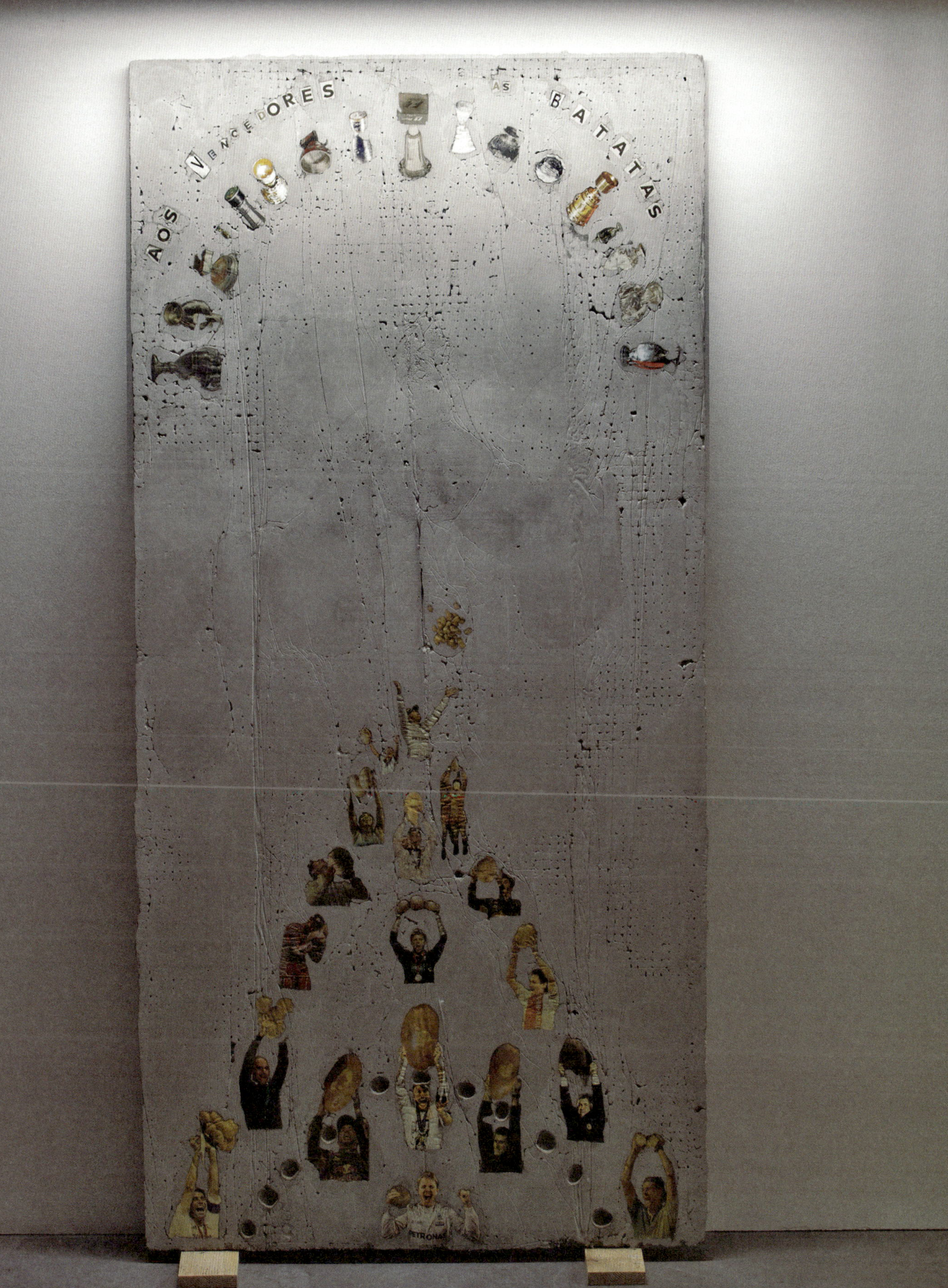
AOS VENCEDORES AS BATATAS

Although Orwell developed these thoughts at a very specific moment in time, basic parallels can nevertheless be discussed between sporting and military struggle. For instance, the resumption of the Olympic tradition in the modern era was expressly motivated by the idea of transferring national competitions from the battlefield to the sports field – essentially shifting from one to the other – as the founding father of the IOC, Pierre de Coubertin, intended.[5] The inherent mechanisms and hierarchies of victory and defeat are closely related in sport and war. One might ask which is the continuation of which by other means? In any case, in terms of etymology and art history, the trophies to be won date back to ancient Greek war methods. The tropaion, in architecture, refers to a victory monument which was built on the site of a battle. In its oldest original form, the weapons of the defeated were hung on trees; this served to convey superiority and discourage potential enemies. A comparable visual symbolism can also be found, for example, in the iconography of triumphal arches.

With his work *For the winners the potatoes*, Rocha Pitta develops his very own approach to the practice of commemoration by exposing the absurdity of the pathos of victory on his concrete slabs. Using strategies of appropriation, decontextualisation and repetition, he not only symbolically empties the trophies, for instance when they are hung upside down and the potatoes pour out onto the jubilant athletes, as shown on his welcoming slab (*Estela # 19; For the winners the potatoes*) in Künstlerhaus Bethanien, but the frenetic exultation is also ridiculed and seems strangely out of place, when the winners celebrate the spuds. Rocha Pitta's particular habit of maintaining an extensive archive with clippings from daily newspapers, free tabloids and various gazettes collected wherever he is – sorted by gestures and visual languages – adds another element to his compositions, blurring time and place and conveying a universal repertoire of gestures. Apart from twisting reali-

5 Cf. Young, David C.: *The Modern Olympics – A Struggle for Revival*. Baltimore: Johns Hopkins University Press, 1996, p. 68.

Bewohner der Stadt auszusprechen. Es ist nicht die bloße Reklame für den Besuch einer Ausstellung, sondern ein ernst gemeinter Aufruf zur Partizipation. Dies wird dadurch unterstrichen, dass die nicht abgeholten Kartoffeln am Ende eines Tages der Berliner Tafel und somit bedürftigen Personen zugute kommen. Nebenbei bieten die Außenstellen den Passierenden und Wartenden einen überraschenden und skurrilen Moment jenseits des Alltagstrotts, wie sich zur Laufzeit gut beobachten ließ.

Rocha Pittas Installation im Innen- und Außenraum der Stadt lässt sich auf einer abstrakteren Ebene als intervenierende Geste lesen, die gleich mehrere Systeme kapert und kurzschließt. Zunächst eignet er sich in den Betontafeln den internationalen Spitzensport an. George Orwell identifizierte den sportlichen Wettkampf in seinem 1945 veröffentlichten Essay *The Sporting Spirit* als einen Auswuchs des aggressiven Nationalismus, der diesen nur weiter befeuere.[4] Auch wenn Orwell aus einer sehr spezifischen Zeit heraus seine Gedanken verfasste, so lassen sich prinzipielle Parallelen zwischen sportlichen und kriegerischen Auseinandersetzungen diskutieren. Zum Beispiel erfolgte die Wiederaufnahme der olympischen Tradition in der Neuzeit ausdrücklich aus dem Gedanken, nationale Wettkämpfe vom Schlachtfeld auf den Sportplatz zu verlegen – also eine Verschiebung vorzunehmen – wie es sich der Gründungsvater des IOC, Pierre de Coubertin, wünschte.[5] Die inhärenten Wirkmechanismen und Hierarchien des Siegens und Verlierens in Sport und Krieg sind eng miteinander verwandt. Man könnte fragen, was wessen Fortsetzung mit anderen Mitteln ist. Die zu gewinnenden Trophäen gehen jedenfalls ihrer Wortherkunft nach sowie kunsthistorisch auf alt-griechische Kriegspraktiken zurück. Das Tropaion bezeichnet in der Architektur ein Siegesdenkmal, das an dem Ort einer Schlacht erreichtet wurde. Die ursprünglichste Form bestand aus den an Bäumen aufgehängten

4 Vgl. www.orwell.ru/library/articles/spirit/english/e_spirit (abgerufen am 2.3.2017)

5 Vgl. Young, David C.: *The Modern Olympics – A Struggle for Revival*. Baltimore: Johns Hopkins University Press, 1996, S. 68.

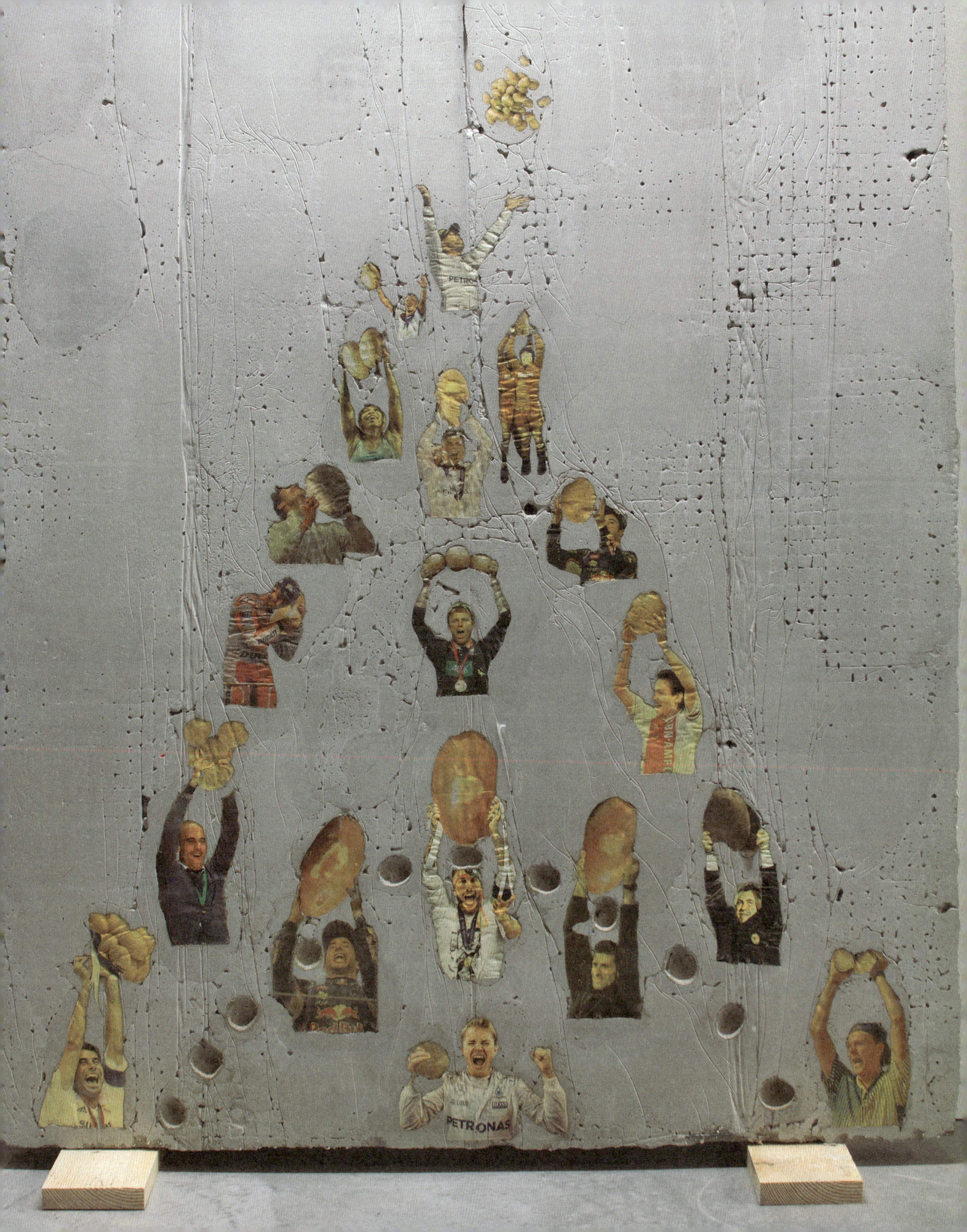
PETRONAS

ties in an amusing way, Rocha Pitta's concrete collages reveal yet another layer of meaning, which contributes to the destabilisation of the system thus invaded. The illustrated concrete slabs may at first seem to resemble the panels in Aby Warburg's picture atlas *Mnemosyne*. Yet in contrast to the atlas no mobility is intended for the opposing pictorial worlds. Rocha Pitta is not concerned with retracing a regional, temporal, social or cultural transformation of stereotypical expressions, but rather, figuratively speaking, aims to set the collision of different gestures in stone, allowing for new levels of meaning to unfold from the synaesthetic intellectual leap between them. In this context, Michael Asbury has noted an interesting parallel between the work of Rocha Pitta and Antonio Manuel, who is also from Brazil.[6] Manuel was one of the few artists who did not leave the country during the military dictatorship between 1964 and 1985. The appropriation of production methods is typical of his approach; for example, he was able to gain access to the printing plates of a large tabloid newspaper and subtly manipulate the images and texts on the title pages, while retaining much of the original content. He then smuggled these modified newspapers into a number of newsagent shops, where they were sold as regular issues. The readers could not distinguish between fiction and reality and were forced to draw their own conclusions on what was true.[7] Rocha Pitta's concrete slabs work on a similar basis; however, he appropriates the contents of newspapers that have already been printed and inserts them into a completely new context. His works in turn look like printing plates which can be used to reproduce new contents. He thereby creates the template for a new narrative that dissolves the original hierarchy of victory and defeat and mounts a challenge to its value, while also deliberately appealing to the escapist-utopian potential and prerogative of art.

6 Cf. Asbury, Michael: *Matheus Rocha Pitta: Brasil*. In: *What Seperates Us*. (Exhibition catalogue) London: HS Projects and Embassy of Brazil, 2016, pp. 35–42.

7 Cf. Munder, Heike (ed.): *Resistance Performed. An Anthology on Aesthetic Strategies under Repressive Regimes in Latin America*. Zurich: Jrp Ringier, 2015, p. 146.

For the winners the potatoes
plastic bags, concrete, glass, bricks and fresh potatoes
variable dimensions
2017

Waffen der Unterlegenen. Es diente dergestalt als Ausdruck der Überlegenheit und Abschreckung potenzieller Feinde. Vergleichbare Bildformeln finden sich beispielsweise auch in der Ikonografie von Triumphbögen.

Rocha Pitta verschiebt mit *For the winners the potatoes* so eine Form des Gedenkens in eine ganz eigene Richtung, indem er auf seinen Betonplatten den Siegespathos ad absurdum führt. Mithilfe der Strategien der Aneignung, Dekontextualisierung und Wiederholung entleert er sinnbildlich nicht nur die Pokale, wenn sie etwa kopfüber hängend Kartoffeln auf die jubelnden Sportler regnen lassen, wie auf der begrüßenden Tafel *(Estela # 19; For the winners the potatoes)* im Künstlerhaus, sondern auch der frenetische Jubel wird dem Spott preisgegeben und wirkt merkwürdig deplatziert, wenn die Gewinnerinnen und Gewinner die Knollen feiern. Rocha Pittas spezifische Angewohnheit, ein umfangreiches Archiv mit Ausschnitten aus Tages- und Gratiszeitungen sowie sonstigen Anzeigenblättern seiner jeweilige Aufenthaltsorte zu pflegen, das nach unterschiedlichen Gesten und Bildsprachen sortiert ist, verleiht seinen Kompositionen eine zusätzliche Komponente, die Ort und Zeit verwischen lässt und einem universellen Gestenrepertoire Ausdruck verleiht. Neben diesem vergnüglichen Verdrehen der Realitäten offenbaren Rocha Pittas Betoncollagen noch eine weitere Ebene, die zur Destabilisierung des so geenterten Systems beiträgt. Anders als bei Aby Warburgs Tafeln zum Bilderatlas *Mnemosyne*, an welche die illustrierten Betonplatten zunächst erinnern könnten, ist keine Beweglichkeit der gegensätzlichen Bildwelten intendiert. Rocha Pitta geht es nicht darum, eine regionale, temporale, soziale oder kulturelle Transformation formelhafter Ausdrücke nachzuvollziehen, sondern vielmehr die Kollision unterschiedlicher Gesten sprichwörtlich in Stein zu meißeln,

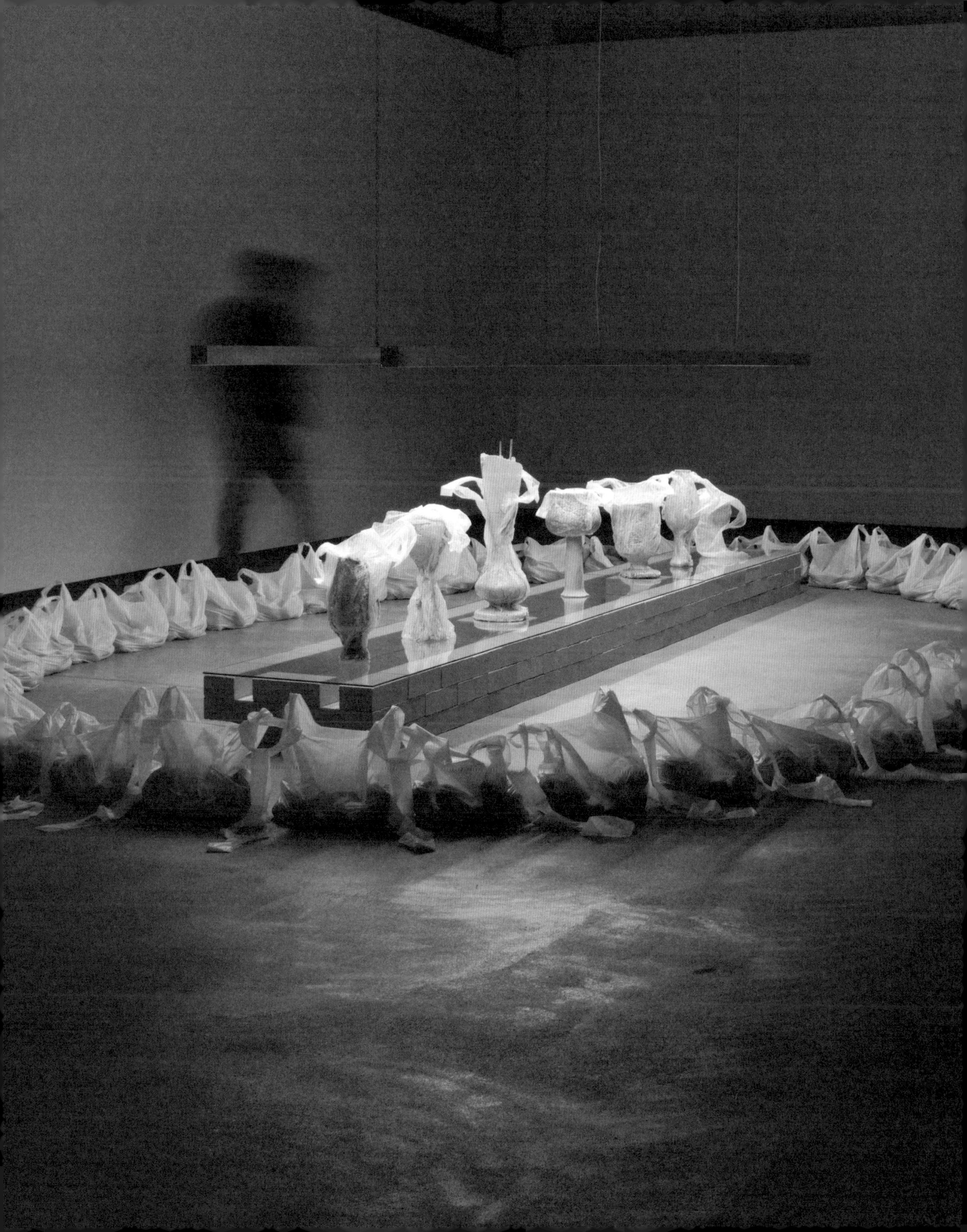

With a further act of intervention the artist usurps a second system, namely art itself, in order to create new links. In his exhibition, Rocha Pitta deals with the two formative poles – ownership and power – which are particularly evident in this sphere,[8] and overturns them. According to the title *For the winners the potatoes*, everyone can be a winner here. Simply by picking up a single potato, anybody can leave the room as a winner. On a conceptual level, the performative gesture of empowerment extends to the thousands of people who benefit from the services of the charity association Berliner Tafel, which receives the potatoes in the evening. In this way, Rocha Pitta turns the exhibition space into a place of participation, where the usual roles of the works of art and the audience – as well as of exclusion and inclusion – are disrupted and the ritual process of viewing switches to touching and taking away. The White Cube is also formally transformed into a place that brings people together by the almost concentric installation. In a chapter of his book *Masters of Truth in Archaic Greece*, Marcel Detienne describes the emergence of community and the public by reference to several original rites such as athletic competitions, consultative meetings or the distribution of trophies looted in war. He concludes that a singular spatial model was decisive for such events: a circular-centric arrangement in which the distance between each participant ideally was the same. Everything within this formation was common property or concerned the community, including the speeches.[9] Rocha Pitta's layout, with the trophies made from concrete placed in the centre, works in a similar way. The trophies relate to the potatoes around them as

8 In his book *Siegerkunst: Neuer Adel, teure Lust*, Wolfgang Ullrich depicts the reintroduction of feudal power structures into the art market. According to him, the exploding prices for certain works of contemporary art cannot be explained by an increased interest in their content, but by the desire of the so-called social winners to distinguish themselves from others, more precisely the super-rich who wish to distance themselves from the masses by buying art and demonstrate their power by paying sums far removed from reality. Cf. Ullrich, Wolfgang: *Siegerkunst: Neuer Adel, teure Lust*. Berlin: Wagenbach Verlag, 2016.

9 Cf. Detienne, Marcel: *The Masters of Truth in Archaic Greece*. New York: Zone Books 1999.

so dass aus dem synästhetischen Gedankensprung zwischen ihnen neue Bedeutungsebenen erwachsen können. In diesem Zusammenhang hat Michael Asbury eine interessante Parallele zwischen Rocha Pittas und den Arbeiten Antonio Manuels, der ebenfalls aus Brasilien stammt, festgestellt.[6] Manuel war einer der wenigen Künstler, die während der Militärdiktatur zwischen 1964 und 1985 nicht das Land verließen. Typisch für seine Vorgehensweise ist die Aneignung von Produktionsmethoden. So konnte er sich Zugang zu den Druckplatten einer großen Boulevardzeitung verschaffen, um subtile Manipulationen an den Bild- und Textsetzungen der Titelblätter vorzunehmen, wobei er einen Großteil des ursprünglichen Inhalts beibehielt. Diese modifizierten Zeitungen schmuggelte er in einige Kioske, wo sie als reguläre Ausgaben verkauft wurden. Die Leserinnen und Leser konnten nicht zwischen Fiktion und Realität unterscheiden und mussten sich ihr eigenes Bild von der Wahrheit machen.[7] Rocha Pittas Betontafeln funktionieren nach einem ähnlichen Prinzip. Er eignet sich jedoch den bereits gedruckten Zeitungsinhalt an, um ihn in eine neue Anordnung zu bringen. Seine Arbeiten wirken ihrerseits wieder wie Druckplatten, mithilfe derer neue Inhalte reproduziert werden können. Er kreiert auf diese Weise die Vorlage für eine neue Erzählung, die die ursprüngliche Hierarchie von Sieg und Niederlage auflöst und ihren Wert in Frage stellt – sehr bewusst setzt er dabei auf das eskapistisch-utopische Potenzial und Vorrecht der Kunst.

Mit einem weiteren Akt der Intervention eignet sich der Künstler ein zweites System an, um es kurzzuschließen, nämlich jenes der Kunst selbst. Rocha Pitta thematisiert mit seiner Ausstellung die beiden strukturbestimmenden Pole Besitz und Macht, die in diesem Feld besonders

6 Vgl. Asbury, Michael: *Matheus Rocha Pitta: Brasil*. In: What Seperates Us. (Ausstellungskatalog) London: HS Projects und Embassy of Brazil, 2016, S. 35–42.

7 Vgl. Munder, Heike (Hrsg.): *Resistance Performed. An Anthology on Aesthetic Strategies under Repressive Regimes in Latin America*. Zürich: Jrp Ringier, 2015, S. 146.

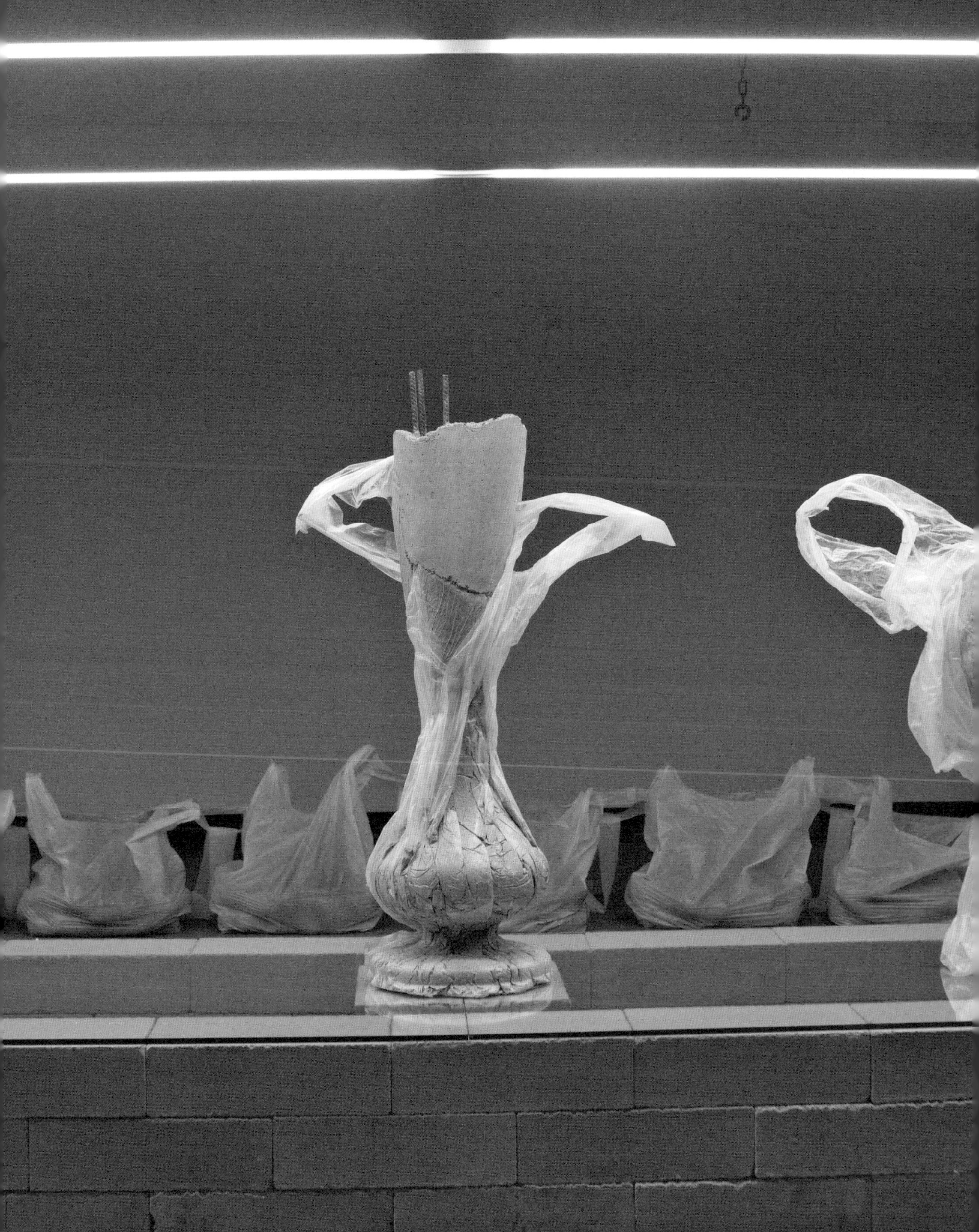

well as to the visitors, who upon entering automatically become part of the artwork and, by performing a simple action, are included in an undefined circle of winners.

The artist's installation not only subverts expectations of art, of visitors and of the institution, but also disrupts two distinct value chains and puts the spotlight on them. On the one hand, helped by the funds provided for the exhibition, he overturns the value chain of the general market economy by daily transforming large quantities of potatoes into temporary art objects – trophies – and spreading them out without any competition or anything in return in an archaic democratic gesture like spoils of war. In fact, blood sticks to the imperial spud; it was brought to Europe from South America in the 16th century by the Spanish conquistadores.

On the other hand, Rocha Pitta undermines the production of value in the art world, which mainly derives from two sources: originality and scarcity. Taking a potato cannot satisfy any art collector or make a speculator rich in the secondary market – the object presented is too profane, too ephemeral, too general.

A fertile common ground between the two systems connected by the artist arises from the fact that both sports and the world of art are classic examples of so-called "winner-take-all" markets; a competitive environment in which a tiny difference in product or service leads to a disproportionately large difference in reward in that particular field. A result of this game of all or nothing is a void in the middle, a phenomenon that in a metaphorical sense currently applies to many aspects of our life in society. In contrast, Rocha Pitta's *For the winners the potatoes* displays an utopian antithesis. With ease and plenty of humour he declares that we are all winners – neither defining too clearly what sort of competition we are in, nor stating exactly what this victory means or whether there are any losers. Although by implementing artistic strategies of participatory performativity, appropriation of infrastructures, dematerialisation and

deutlich zu Tage treten[8], und hebelt diese aus. Dem Titel *For the winners the potatoes* zufolge kann hier jeder zum Sieger werden. Allein das Auflesen einer einzigen Kartoffel führt dazu, dass man als Gewinner den Raum verlässt. Die performative Ermächtigungsgeste überträgt sich konzeptionell weiter auf die Tausenden von Menschen, welche die Berliner Tafel in Anspruch nehmen, an die die Kartoffeln am Abend weitergegeben werden. Dergestalt transformiert er den Ausstellungsraum zu einem Ort der Teilhabe, in dem die übliche Rollenverteilung von Werk und Publikum – auch von Exklusion und Inklusion – aufgehoben wird und das rituelle Betrachten in ein Anfassen und Mitnehmen verdreht wird. Die nahezu konzentrische Installation verwandelt den White Cube auch formal zu einem Ort des Miteinanders. Marcel Detienne beschreibt in einem Kapitel seines Buchs *Masters of Truth in Archaic Greece* das Entstehen von Gemeinschaft und Öffentlichkeit anhand mehrerer ursprünglicher Riten wie den athletischen Wettkämpfen, beratenden Versammlungen oder dem Verteilen der im Krieg erbeuteten Trophäen. Er kommt zu dem Schluss, dass ein singuläres Raummodell bestimmend für derlei Institutionen war, nämlich eine kreisförmige zentrierte Anordnung, in der idealerweise jeder Beteiligte im gleichen Abstand zueinander stand. Alles innerhalb dieser Formation war Gemeingut oder betraf die Gemeinschaft, ebenso auch Redebeiträge.[9] In vergleichbarer Weise funktioniert Rocha Pittas Konstellation, in deren Mitte die aus Beton gegossenen Trophäen platziert sind. Sie betreffen die um sie befindlichen Kartoffeln ebenso wie die Besucherinnen und Besucher, die mit Betreten automatisch Teil der Arbeit und durch das Ausführen

8 Wolfgang Ullrich schildert in seinem Buch Siegerkunst: *Neuer Adel, teure Lust* das Wiedereinziehen feudaler Machtstrukturen in den Kunstmarkt. Ihm zufolge lassen sich die explodierenden Preise für bestimmte Werke zeitgenössischer Kunst nicht etwa durch ein gesteigertes inhaltliches Interesse erklären, sondern durch den Distinktionswillen sogenannter gesellschaftlicher Sieger–Superreiche, die sich mit dem Kauf von Kunst von der Masse absetzen wollen und mit dem Zahlen realitätsferner Summen ihre Macht demonstrieren. Vgl. Ullrich, Wolfgang: Siegerkunst: *Neuer Adel, teure Lust*. Berlin: Wagenbach Verlag, 2016.

9 Vgl. Detienne, Marcel: *The Masters of Truth in Archaic Greece*. New York: Zone Books 1999.

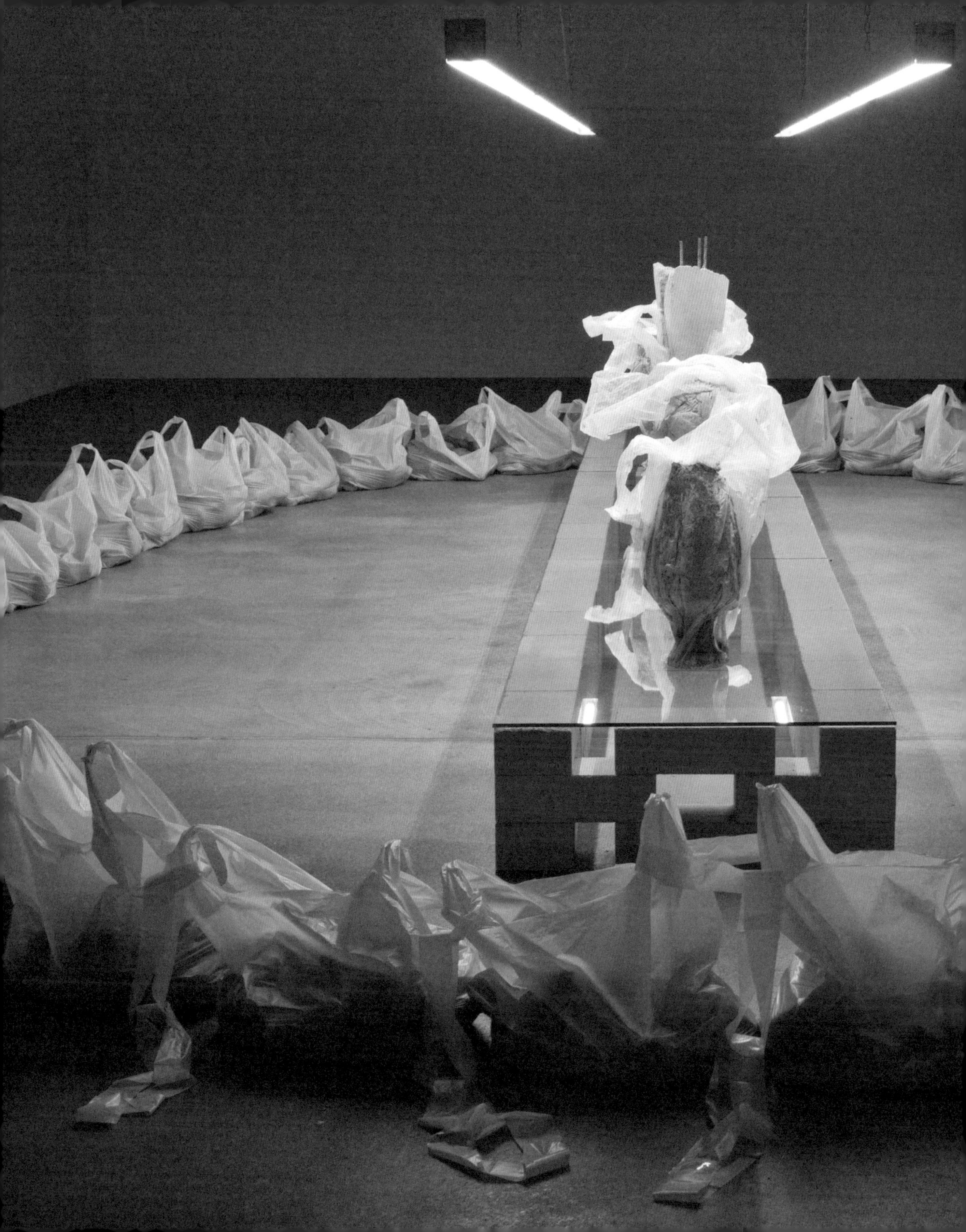

the recreation of links between art and life he is rooted in the tradition of conceptual art, which had a particular political importance in South America during the various repressive systems of government from the 1960s to the 1980s, Rocha Pitta operates from a different perspective and with a different self-confidence. In an interview that was published shortly before the exhibition, he commented:

“I don't think art can change anything. I don't think art is important for practical matters. Art is a way to make you sane, to make sense of things. There is something in art that is very escapist, or the idea of political art, because usually you want to forget reality, you want to change the subject.“[10]

Therefore, it is only logical that *For the winners the potatoes* in the end does not spell out the moral of the story, and neither does the novel. Rocha Pitta creates a many-faceted visual world, in which we ourselves become participants. He gives some clues, leaves traces, confronts us with the familiar in unusual settings and vice versa, and takes us on a labyrinthine journey leading from trivial thoughts about what to cook for dinner with our potatoes to issues that affect the core of our life in society. But he does not push us too far, beyond the turning point of the graphically staged parable, which represents the link between what is said and what is meant. He leaves it up to us to find answers to the question of what it means when the winners pocket the potatoes. Let us hope that we will fare better than Rubião.

10 www.artberlin.de/matheus-rocha-pitta/ (accessed 14.03.2017)

einer simplen Handlung auch in einen nicht näher bestimmten Kreis von Siegern aufgenommen werden.

Rocha Pittas Installation betreibt nicht nur ein Verwirrspiel mit den Erwartungshaltungen an die Kunst, die Besucher und die Institution, sondern er unterbricht auch zweierlei Wertschöpfungsketten und hebt sie hervor: zum einen eine allgemeine marktwirtschaftliche, indem er täglich mithilfe des Ausstellungsbudgets große Mengen Kartoffeln zu temporären Kunstobjekten – Trophäen – transformiert und diese ohne Wettbewerb oder Gegenleistung in einer archaisch demokratischen Geste wie Kriegsbeute ausbreitet – tatsächlich klebt Blut an der imperialen Knolle, kam sie doch im 16. Jahrhundert durch die spanischen Konquistadoren von Südamerika nach Europa.

Zum anderen unterläuft Rocha Pitta die Wertproduktion im Kunstfeld, die sich zu großen Teilen aus Originalität und Verknappung speist. Das Mitnehmen einer Kartoffel kann keinen Kunstsammler befriedigen oder einen Spekulanten auf dem Sekundärmarkt reich machen – zu profan, zu ephemer, zu allgemein ist der dargebotene Gegenstand.

Eine fruchtbare Gemeinsamkeit beider vom Künstler kurzgeschlossener Systeme besteht darin, dass es sich sowohl beim Sport als auch dem Kunstfeld um klassische Beispiele für sogenannte Winner-take-all-Märkte handelt; ein Wettbewerb, in dem ein Produkt oder eine Dienstleistung mit nur minimalem Vorteil gegenüber der Konkurrenz einen unverhältnismäßig hohen Anteil des Ertrags auf dem jeweiligen Feld gewinnt. Eine Konsequenz dieses Spiels um Alles oder Nichts ist das Fehlen einer Mitte, was sich im Übertragenen als Phänomen derzeit zunehmend in vielen Aspekten unseres Zusammenlebens beobachten lässt. Rocha Pittas *For the winners the potatoes* steht demgegenüber als utopische Antithese im Raum. Mit reichlich Humor und leichtfüßig erklärt er uns alle zu Gewinnern, wobei er weder zu deutlich formuliert,

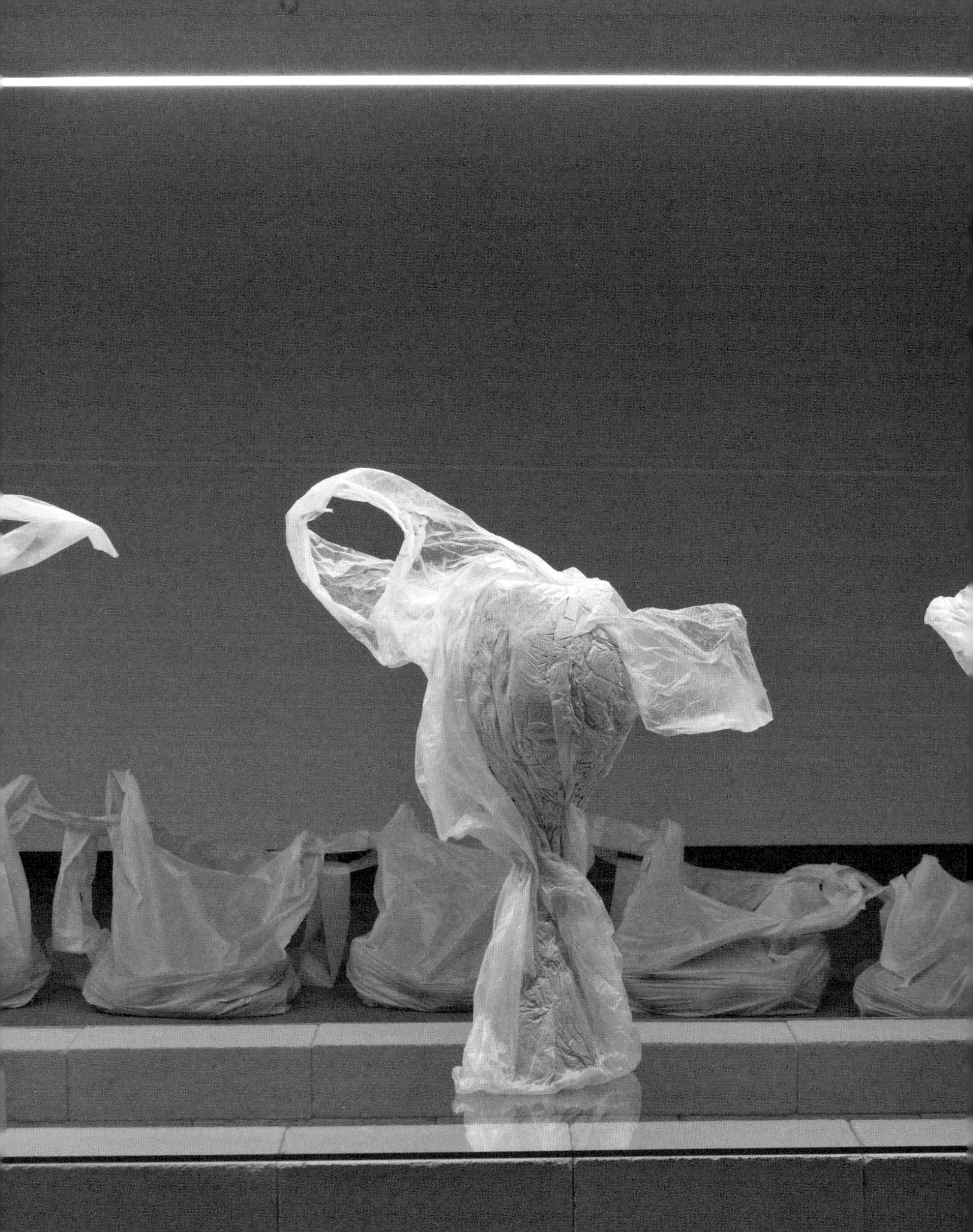

in welchem Wettbewerb wir genau stehen, noch, was dieser Sieg genau bedeutet oder ob es auch Verlierer gibt. Gleichwohl er mit den angewandten künstlerischen Strategien der partizipativen Performativität, Appropriation von Infrastrukturen, der Rückkopplung der Kunst ans Leben und der Dematerialisierung in Tradition der Konzeptkunst steht, die in Südamerika ein besonderes politisches Gewicht unter den vielfältigen repressiven Staatssystemen der 1960er bis 1980er Jahre hatte, operiert Rocha Pitta aus einer deutlich anderen Perspektive und Selbstverständlichkeit. In einem im Vorfeld der Ausstellung veröffentlichtem Interview gibt er zu bedenken:

„I don't think art can change anything. I don't think art is important for practical matters. Art is a way to make you sane, to make sense of things. There is something in art that is very escapist, or the idea of political art, because usually you want to forget reality, you want to change the subject."[10]

Und so ist es nur konsequent, dass *For the winners the potatoes* die Moral der Geschichte am Ende offen lässt, ebenso wie die im Roman erzählte. Rocha Pitta kreiert eine vielschichtige Bildebene, auf der wir selbst zu Akteuren werden. Er legt eine Reihe von Fährten, hinterlässt Spuren, konfrontiert uns mit Vertrautem in ungewöhnlichen Kontexten und umgekehrt, führt uns auf verschlungenen Pfaden durch triviale Überlegungen über die mögliche Abendessensgestaltung mit den gesammelten Kartoffeln zu Problemen, die den Kern unseres Zusammenlebens betreffen. Aber er stößt uns nicht über den Scheitelpunkt, den Wendepunkt der grafisch dargestellten Parabel hinaus, der das Bindeglied zwischen Erzähltem und Gemeintem darstellt. Er lässt uns mit der Frage alleine, was es bedeutet wenn die Gewinner Kartoffeln erbeuten. Hoffen wir, dass es uns damit besser ergeht als Rubião.

10 www.artberlin.de/matheus-rocha-pitta/ (abgerufen am 14.3.2017)

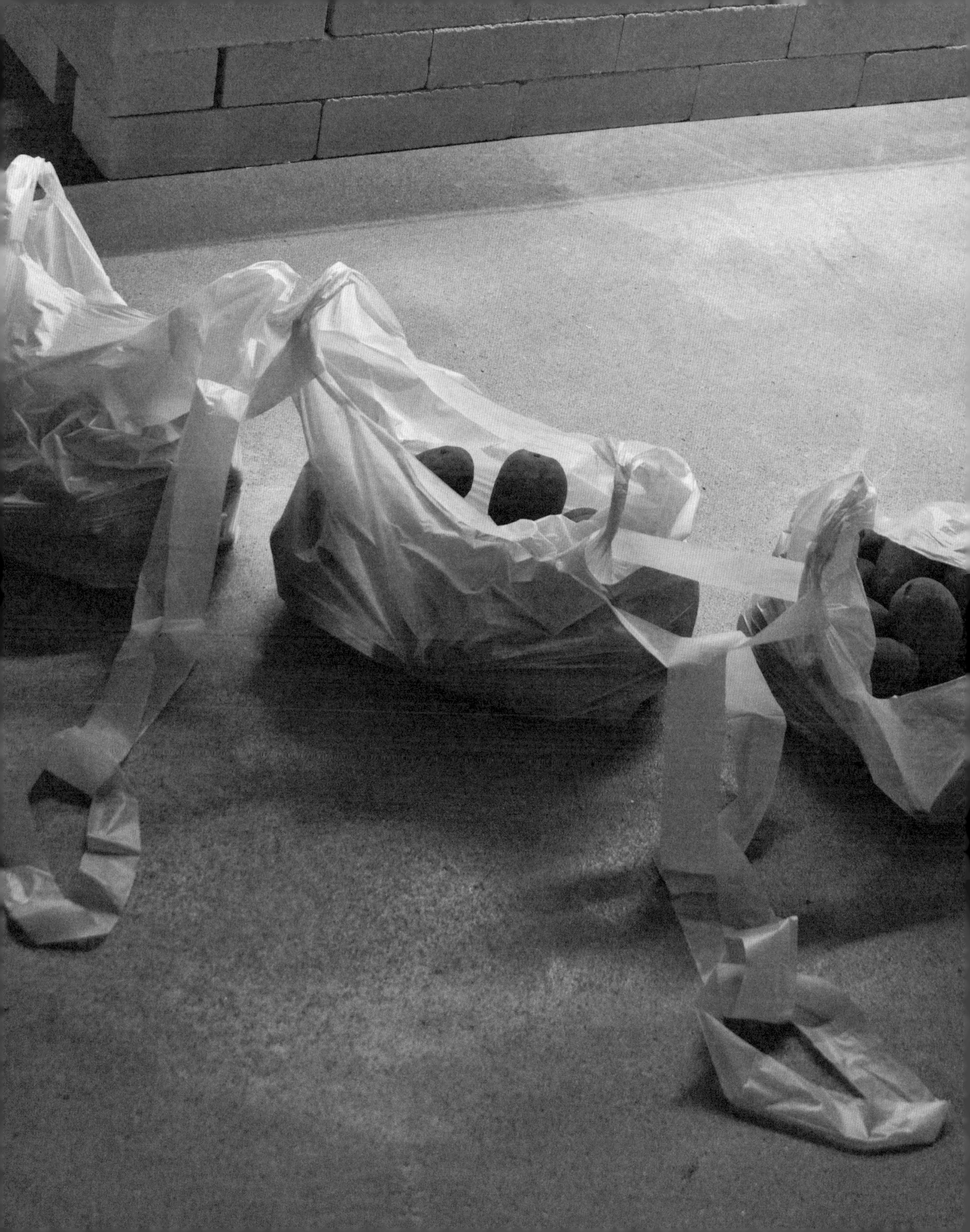

The image shows the tomb of Frederick the Great, known as *'Der Kartoffelkönig' [the Potato King]*, as he reportedly introduced potatoes in Prussia. Nowadays visitors leave potatoes on his tombstone. Photographed by the artist in August 2016 at Sanssouci Palace, Potsdam.

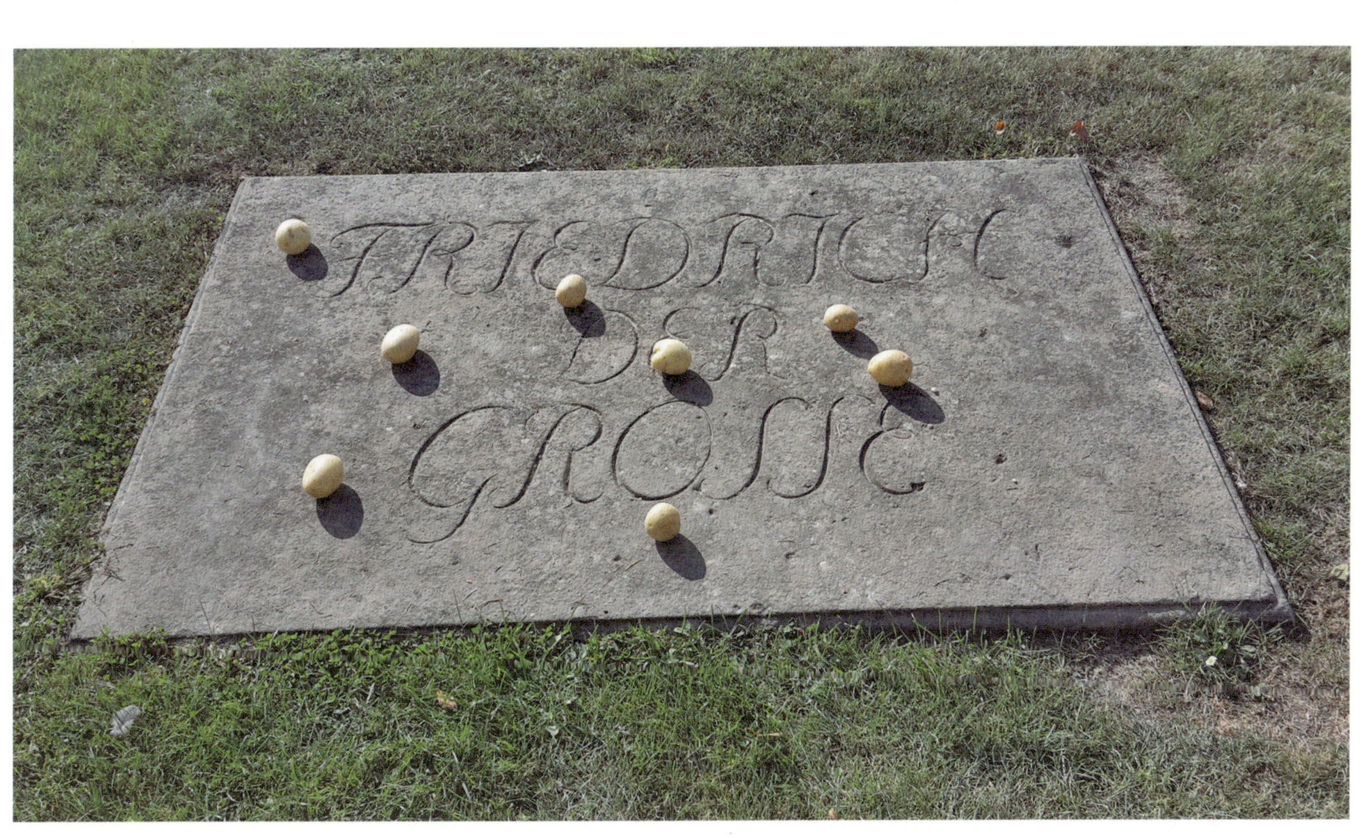
FRIEDRICH
DER
GROSSE

Slabs (Lajes)

The slabs are a series of works that obey quite a simple constructive method: to pair, to confront, to compare newspaper clips (taken from an archive of photos cropped from magazines whose origins go back as far as 2001) with ad images (usually cropped from their "backgrounds", sometimes from packaging as well).

"Laje" in Portuguese denotes both a geological formation and the concrete ceiling of a construction, like the poor brick and cement houses in the favelas.

The technique is a hybrid of collage and casting (a procedure taken from the construction of cheap tombstones in Brazil) where paper is added to the mould, before the wet concrete is poured. When the concrete dries, the paper becomes "walled" instead of pasted.

The result is a delicate dialectic between the promise of advertising and the reality that frustrates it. For example, this slab shows a photograph of refugees travelling in a boat which is contrasted with advertisements for holiday cruises. Similar to the steles and archaeological tablets, it witnesses historical events through the starkly juxtaposed temporalities of publicity and news. This incongruence is also material: the paper fragility shares the same space as the cement brutality.

The slabs have a domestic scale not only in output, but mainly because they are homemade (the moulds come from cardboard boxes found on street markets) and produced in a quotidian time frame.

Slab # 73 (l'aventura)
paper and cement
29 x 40 x 3 cm
2016

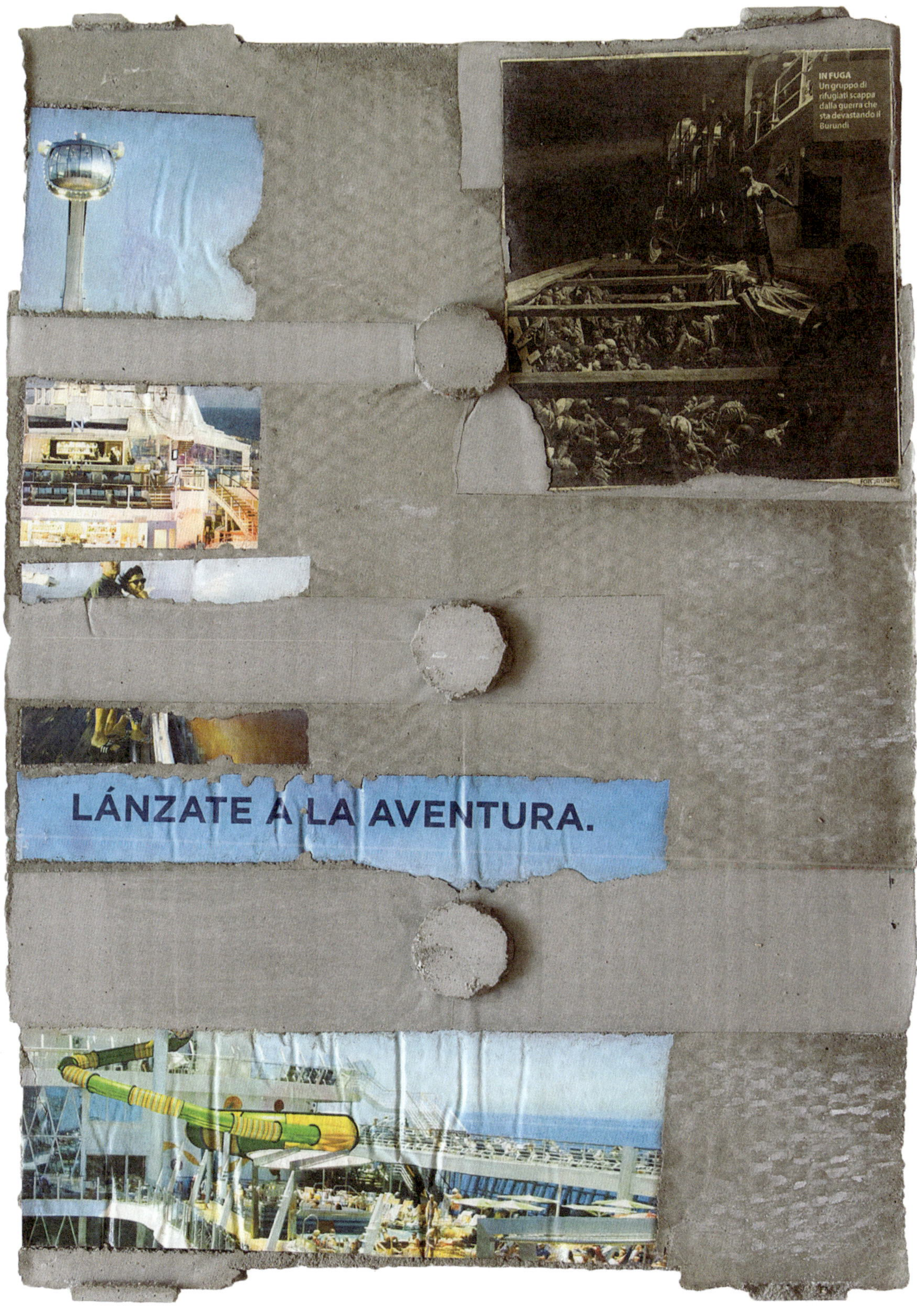
IN FUGA
Un gruppo di rifugiati scappa dalla guerra che sta devastando il Burundi
LÁNZATE A LA AVENTURA.

Detail of *Slab # 19 (Herzog)*

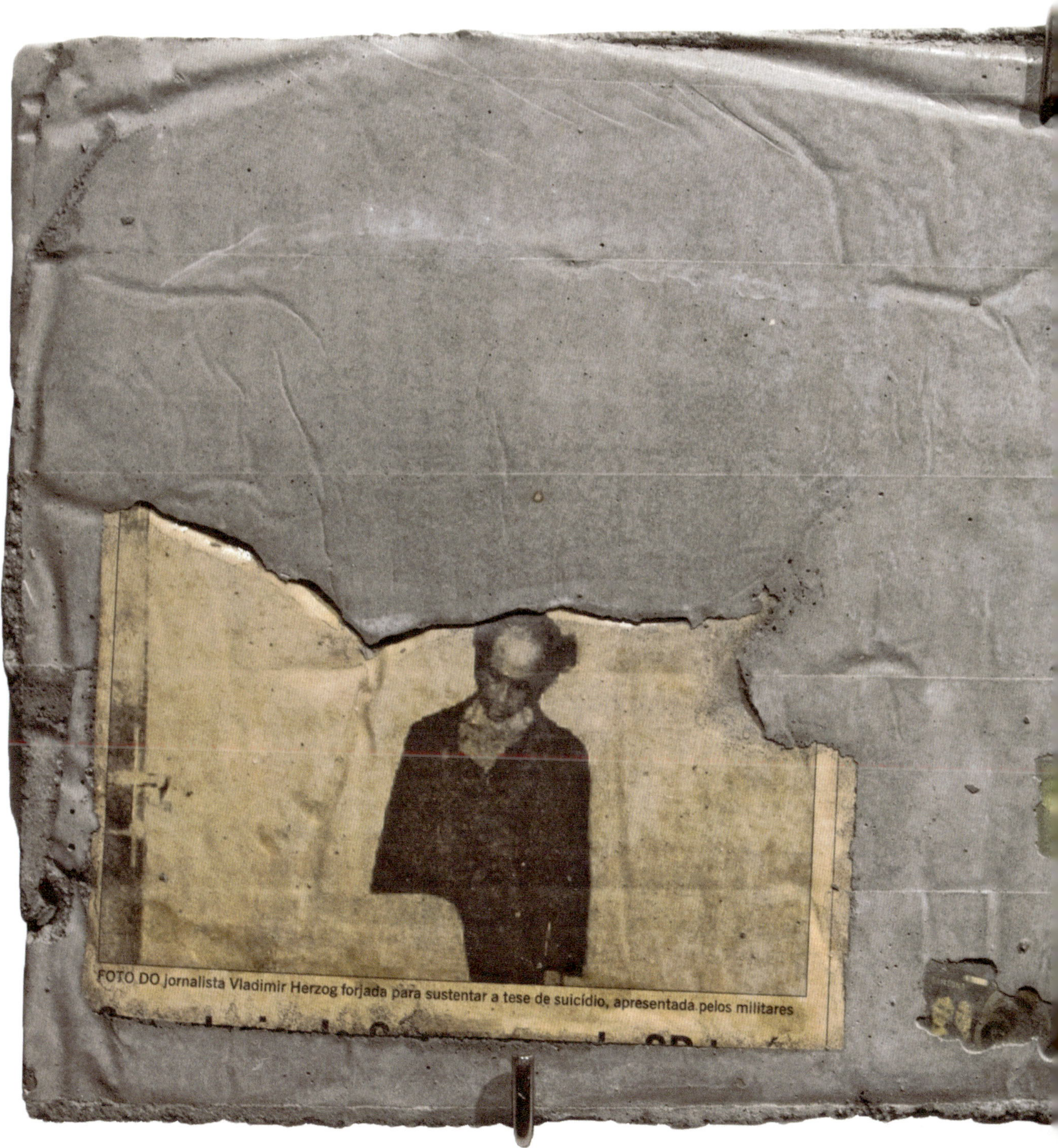
FOTO DO jornalista Vladimir Herzog forjada para sustentar a tese de suicídio, apresentada pelos militares

Slab # 19 (Herzog) has the particularity of being an edition. It was commissioned in 2012 by an editions gallery. I waited patiently for one newspaper edition that would contain all the images to be used in the piece, so I could have ten similar images.

In one edition of 'O Globo', the main newspaper in Rio de Janeiro, I found a piece about Vladimir Herzog, whose death circumstances were brought to public attention by the National Commission of Truth that investigated the human rights violations under the Brazilian dictatorship.

Herzog was a member of the Brazilian Communist Party and was active in the civil resistance movement against the Brazilian military government. In October 1975, Herzog, then editor in chief of TV Cultura, was tortured to death by the political police of the military dictatorship, which later claimed that he had committed suicide. Over 37 years later, his death certificate was revised to say that Herzog had in fact died as a result of torture by the army at DOI-CODI.

In the caption of the photograph one reads: "Photo of the journalist Vladimir Herzog, forged to sustain the suicide thesis, presented by the militaries".

A few pages later, a photograph of an actual army official is presented whose caption is: "Captain Tomás Paiva praised the new equipment tests".

The playful military holding a vigilance device is connected to Herzog's forged image through a diagonal bridge of a small camera, cropped from ads.

Slab # 19 (Herzog)
concrete and paper
44 x 22 x 2 cm
2012

top: edition 9/10
center: edition 7/10
bottom: edition 3/10

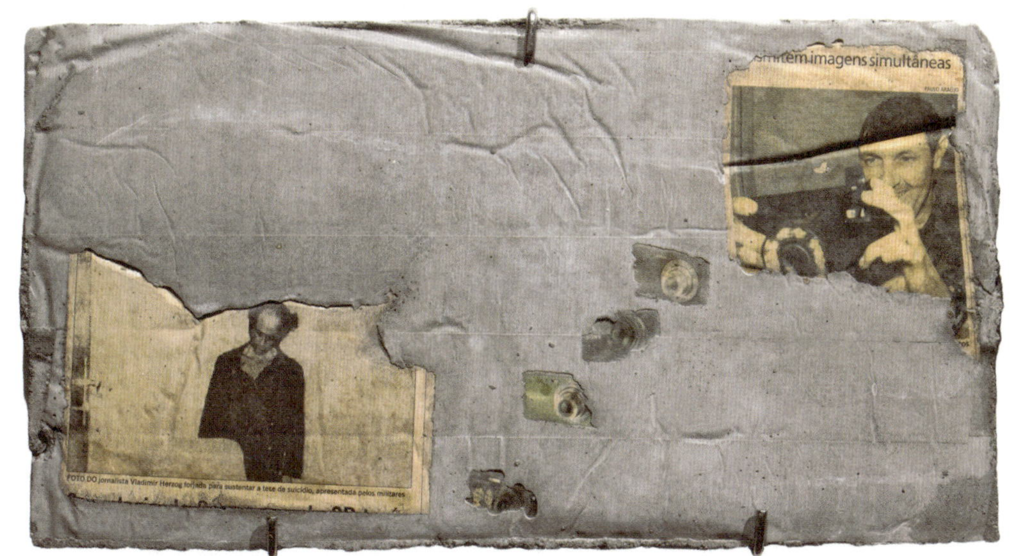
smitem imagens simultâneas
FOTO DO jornalista Vladimir Herzog forjada para sustentar a tese de suicídio, apresentada pelos militares

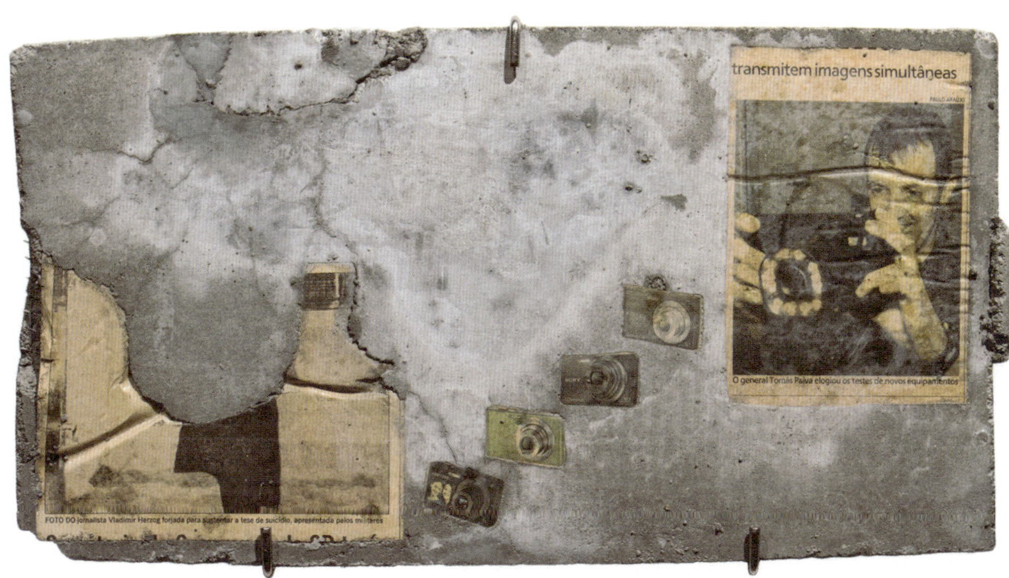
transmitem imagens simultâneas
O general Tomás Paiva elogiou os testes de novos equipamentos
FOTO DO jornalista Vladimir Herzog forjada para sustentar a tese de suicídio, apresentada pelos militares

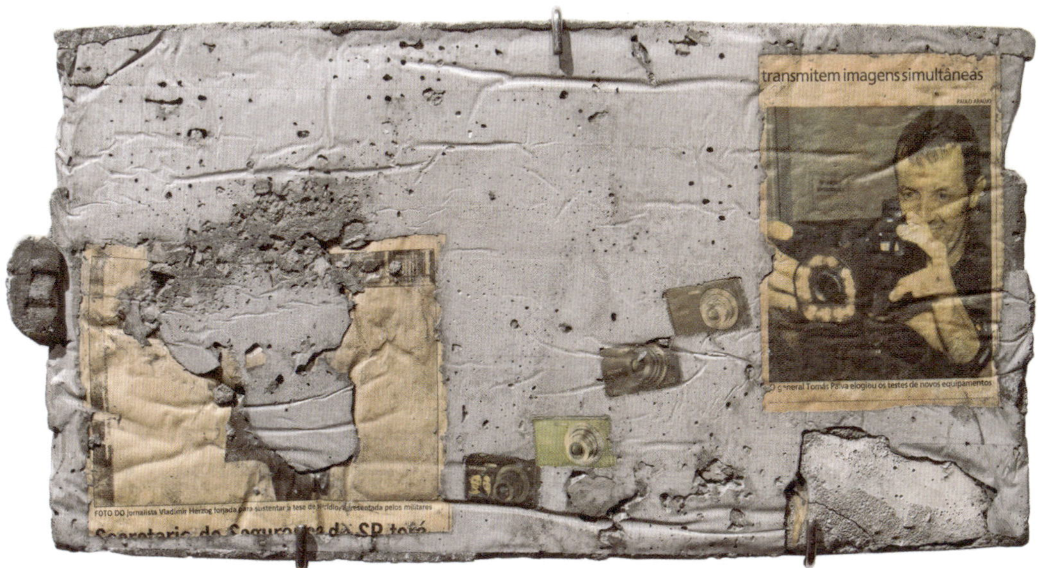
transmitem imagens simultâneas
O general Tomás Paiva elogiou os testes de novos equipamentos

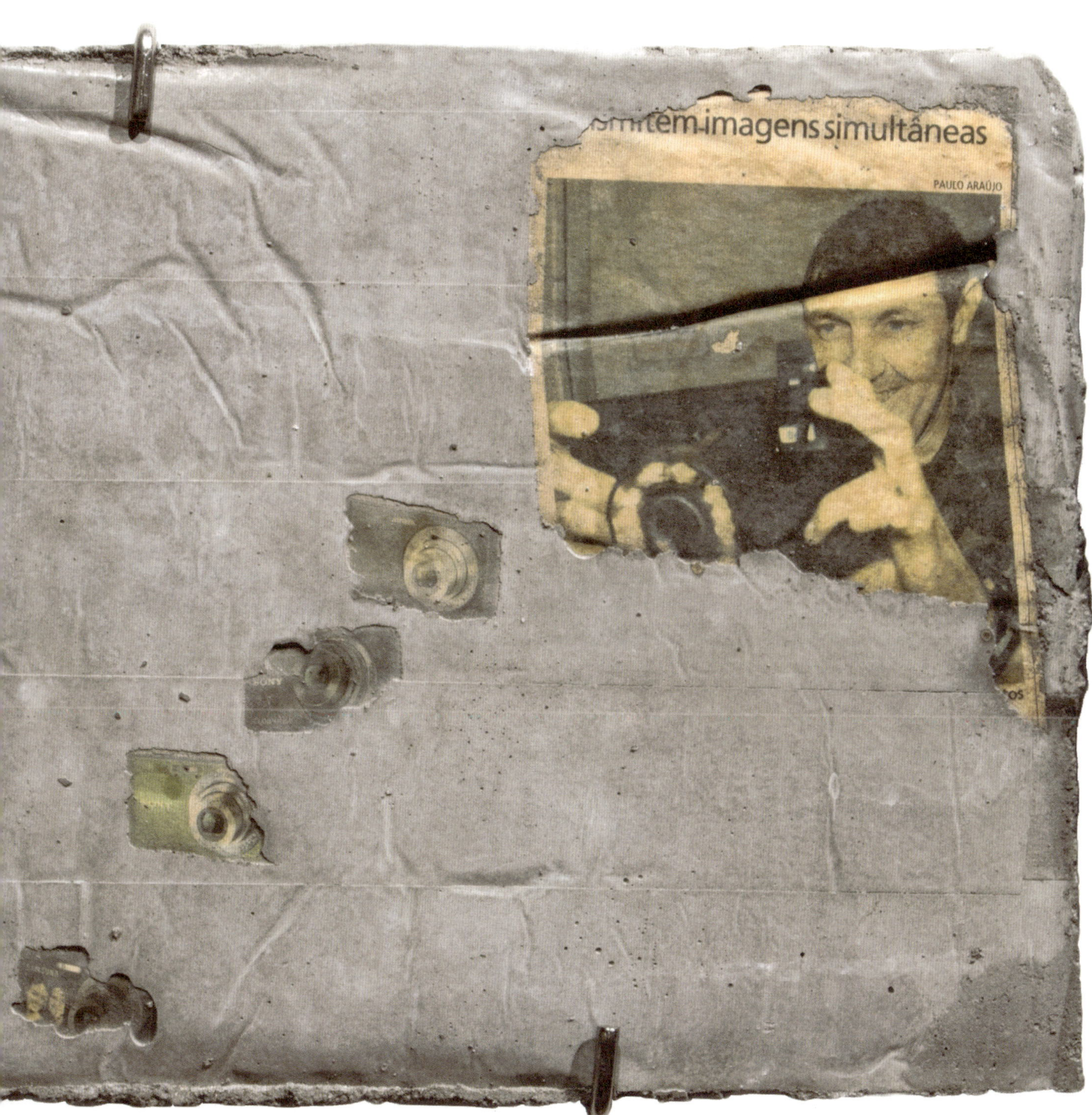
imagens simultâneas
PAULO ARAÚJO

On July 14, 2013, *Amarildo de Souza*, a 43-year-old bricklayer from the Rocinha favela in Rio de Janeiro, Brazil, was called in for questioning by Unidade de Polícia Pacificadora (UPP) officers on his way home from the market. Believed to be connected to drug trafficking activity in the favela, despite having no prior involvement in illegal activity, de Souza was brought in for questioning and was never seen again.

Amarildo was classified as “missing” for more than two months, but increasing public outrage eventually forced the authorities to respond to the suspicious circumstances of his disappearance. By October 2013, twenty-four policemen and UPP commander Edson Santos were accused of torture, concealing a body, procedural fraud and conspiracy. To date, Amarildo's body has not been found. It was determined that he was tortured with electric shocks and suffocated with plastic bags for more than two hours before he was drowned in a bucket.

In the city of Rio, roughly 16% of all registered homicides between 2010 and 2015 were committed by on-duty police officers. As of April 2015, 183 of 220 investigations into police killings were still open, and only one case led to the indictment of a police officer. In this context, de Souza's case became a symbol of the fight against police abuse. “Where is Amarildo?”, served as the rallying call of protesters.

I decided to make Amarildo's stele after finding out that he was famous for carrying two 50 kg bags of cement on his back, the same amount used to do the piece.

Stele # 7 (Amarildo)
concrete, paper and cement packing
180 x 80 x 5 cm
2013

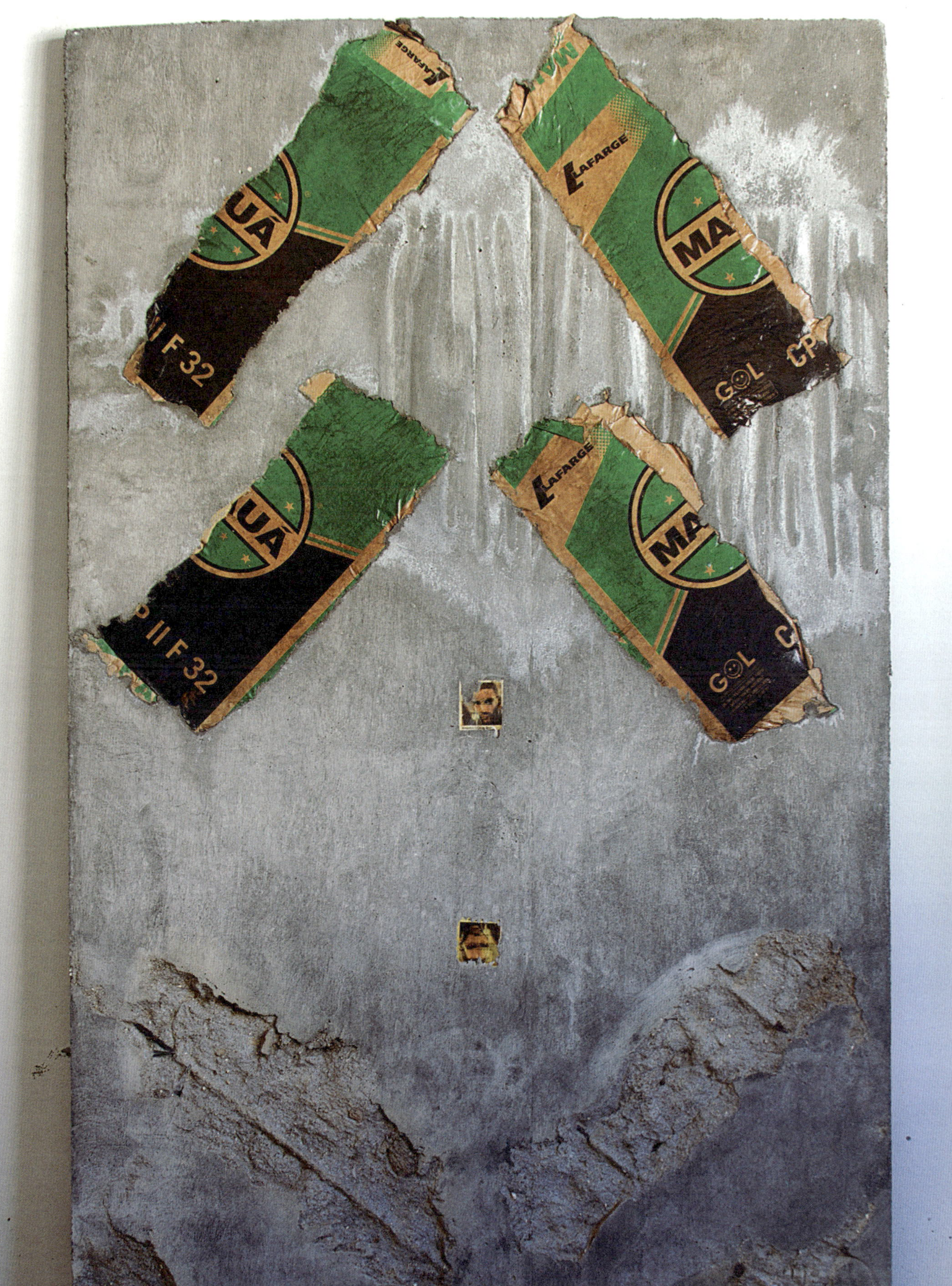
LAFARGE
UÁ
II F 32
LAFARGE
MA
GOL CP
UÁ
P II F 32
LAFARGE
MA
GOL C

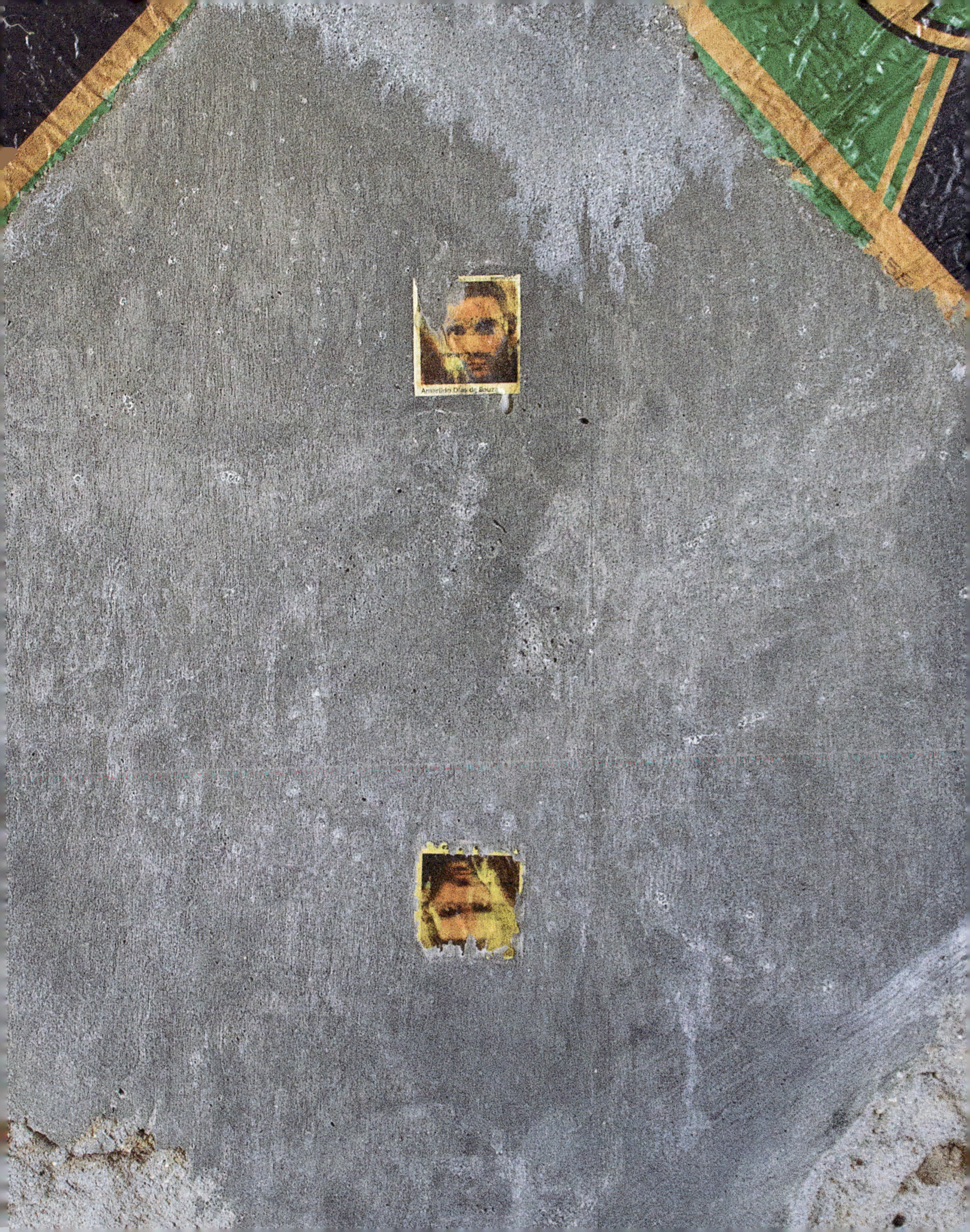

Slab # 75 (first stone)
paper, cement and stone
47,5 x 29,5 x 3 cm
2016

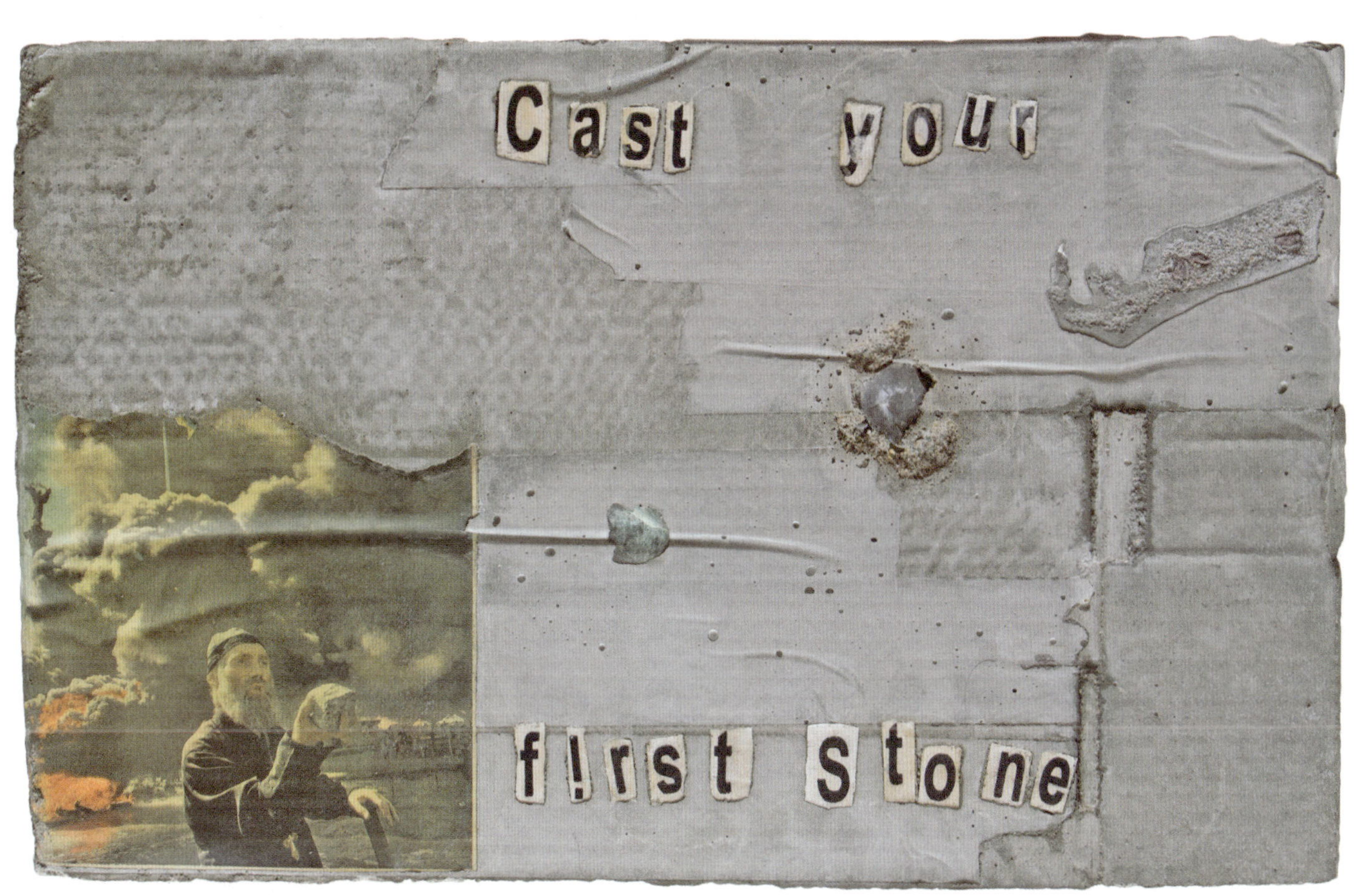
Cast your
first Stone

Slab # 58 (second assault)
concrete and paper
51 x 64,5 x 3 cm
2014

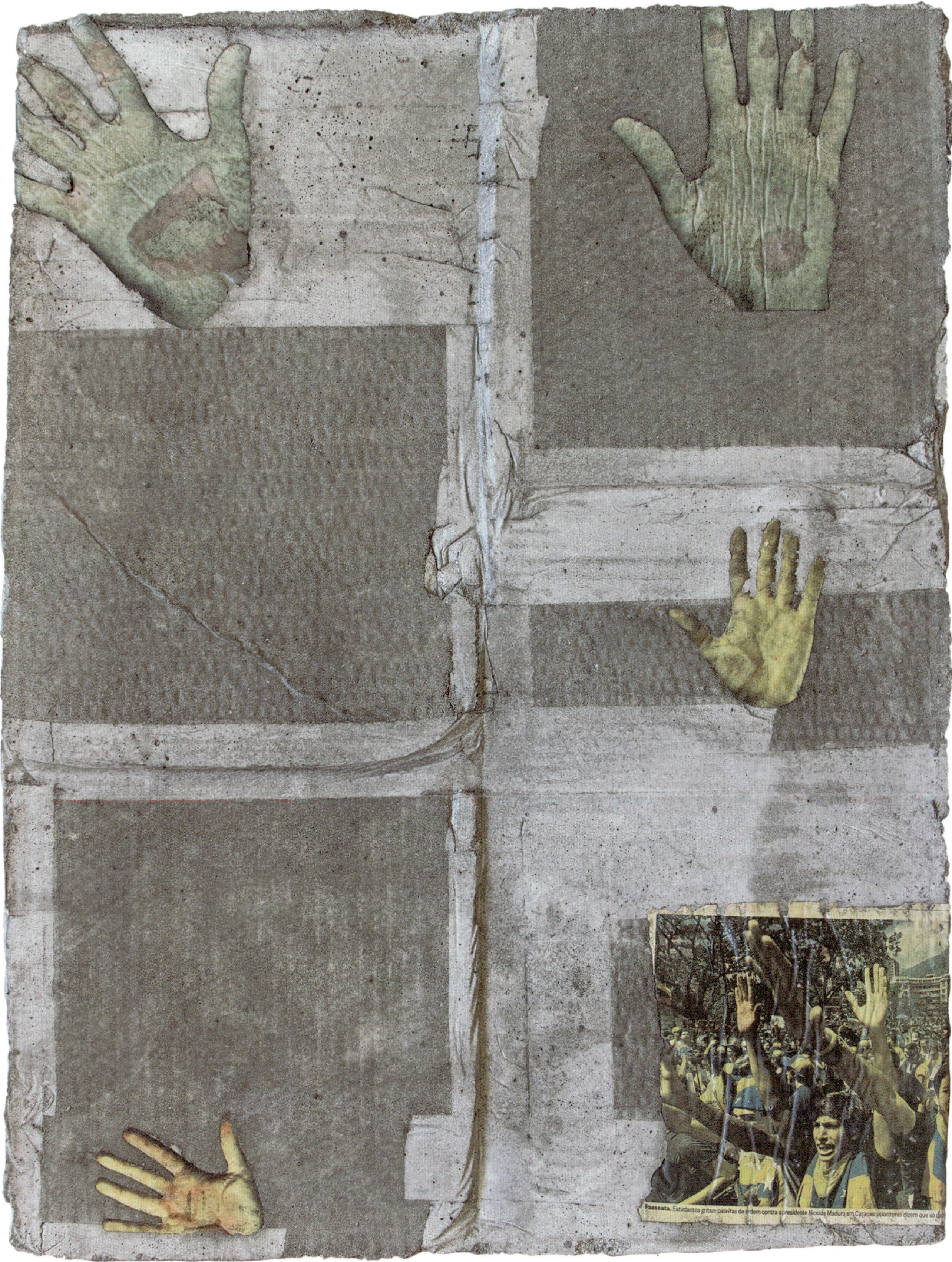
Passeata. Estudantes gritam palavras de ordem contra o presidente Nicolás Maduro em Caracas; opositores dizem que só

The Fool's Year
365 newspaper photographs and 365 printed dates
pasted on Japanese paper
280 x 150 cm
2017
SOX Berlin, April 1, 2017

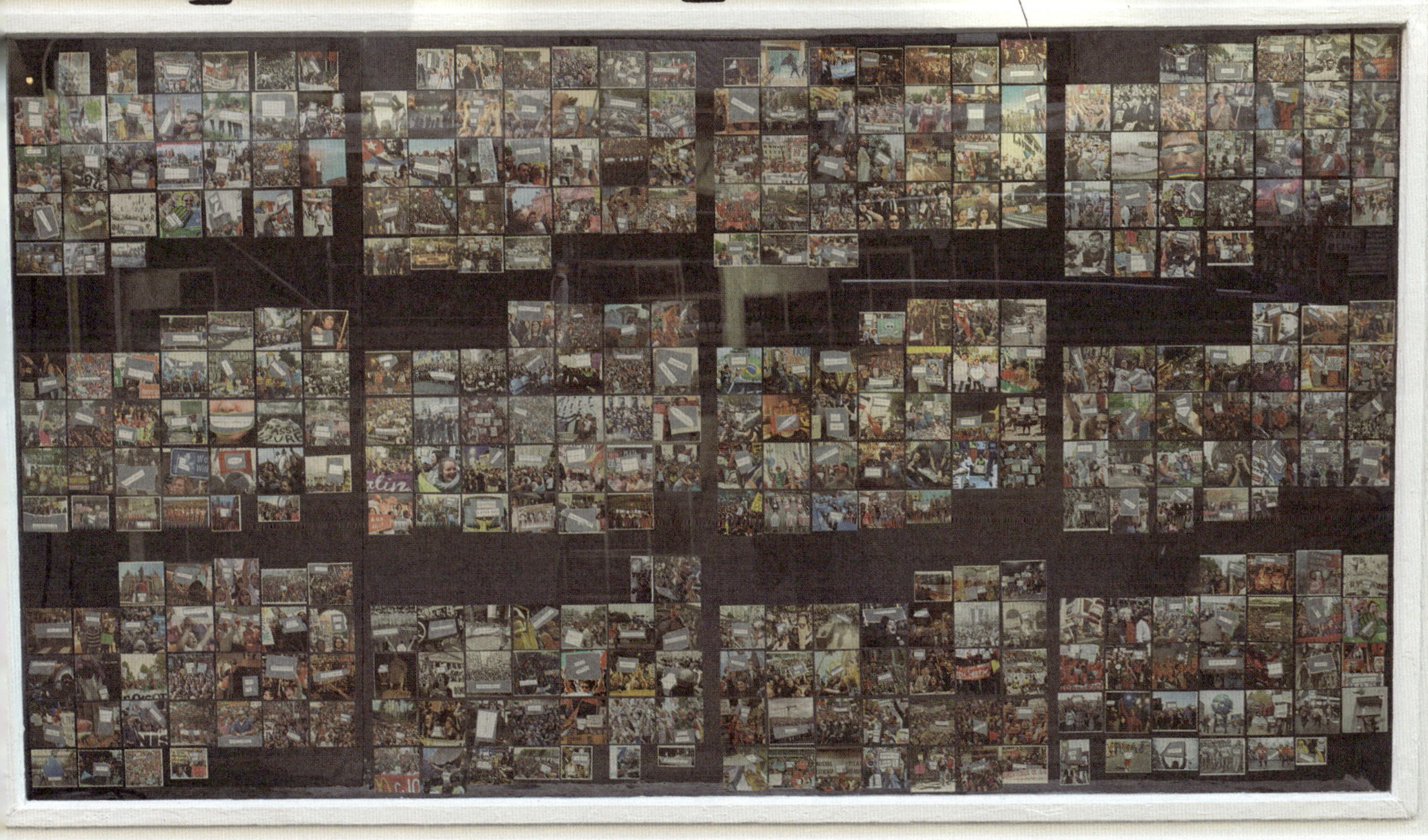
THE FOOL'S YEAR
A CALENDAR BY MATHEUS ROCHA PITTA

The awareness that they are about to make the continuum of history explode is characteristic of the revolutionary classes at the moment of their action. The great revolution introduced a new calendar. The initial day of a calendar serves as a historical time-lapse camera.

Walter Benjamin

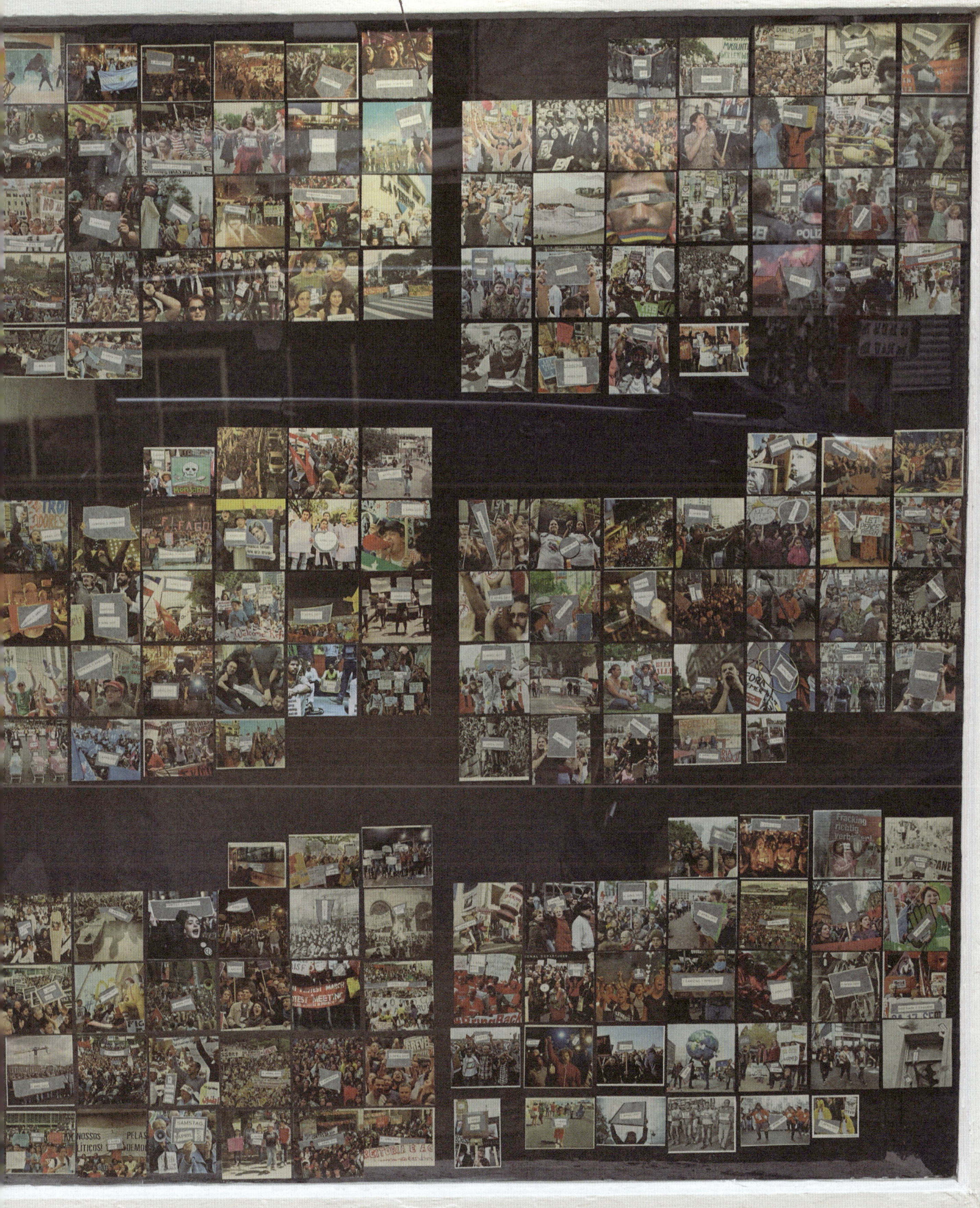

The Fool's Year

by Matheus Rocha Pitta

One of the first things that caught my attention upon my arrival in Berlin were the city's shop windows. Instead of hiring professional designers, shop owners seem to decorate the windows themselves, in a rather amateur, spontaneous and funny way. A copy shop, for example, has a huge display of orchids, whose relationship to printing remains gracefully incomprehensible, unless you imagine the owner's love for these flowers. My installations in the showcases I rented in two underground stations for my exhibition at Künstlerhaus Bethanien are a homage to these adorable, handmade, do-it-yourself displays.

When invited by SOX to use its vitrine on Oranienstraße, right after my opening, I had to respond quickly: as opposed to my project *For the winners the potatoes*, which I developed during my one-year residency, I only had two weeks to come up with something new. Time was short, so I decided to take time as my starting point, to be precise, the day of the opening, April 1st, or Fool's Day.

One reads in the Wikipedia page devoted to it: "In the Middle Ages, New Year's Day was celebrated on March 25 in most European towns. In some areas of France, New Year's was a week-long holiday ending on April 1. Some writers suggest that April Fools' originated because those who celebrated on January 1 made fun of those who celebrated on other dates." So the ones celebrating at another time were regarded as fools – but conversely it exposed the conventions of time measuring.

So Today, on April 1st, here in the street I present *The Fool's Year*, a calendar in which every day is Fool's Day – the entire year condensed and frozen in one single day, or, a single initial day dilated and diluted into a year.

Each and every day is represented by a newspaper photograph of protesters holding posters, banners or flags, whose specific political claim I carefully removed and substituted, early this morning, by the date April 1st, just as it is freshly printed in today's newspapers. These images come from my own archive, which I feed almost every day with newspaper photographs. I love the language of protest, one doesn't need to agree with its content to love it.

So today you see 365 images of protest, 365 days of the past, that claim nothing other than the awareness of Today. For to be regarded as a fool is only a matter of being out of time, of breaking the clocks, as Benjamin cites in his 15th thesis on the concept of history:

Who would have believed it!
We are told that new Joshuas at the foot of every tower,
as though irritated with
time itself, fired at the dials
in order to stop the day.

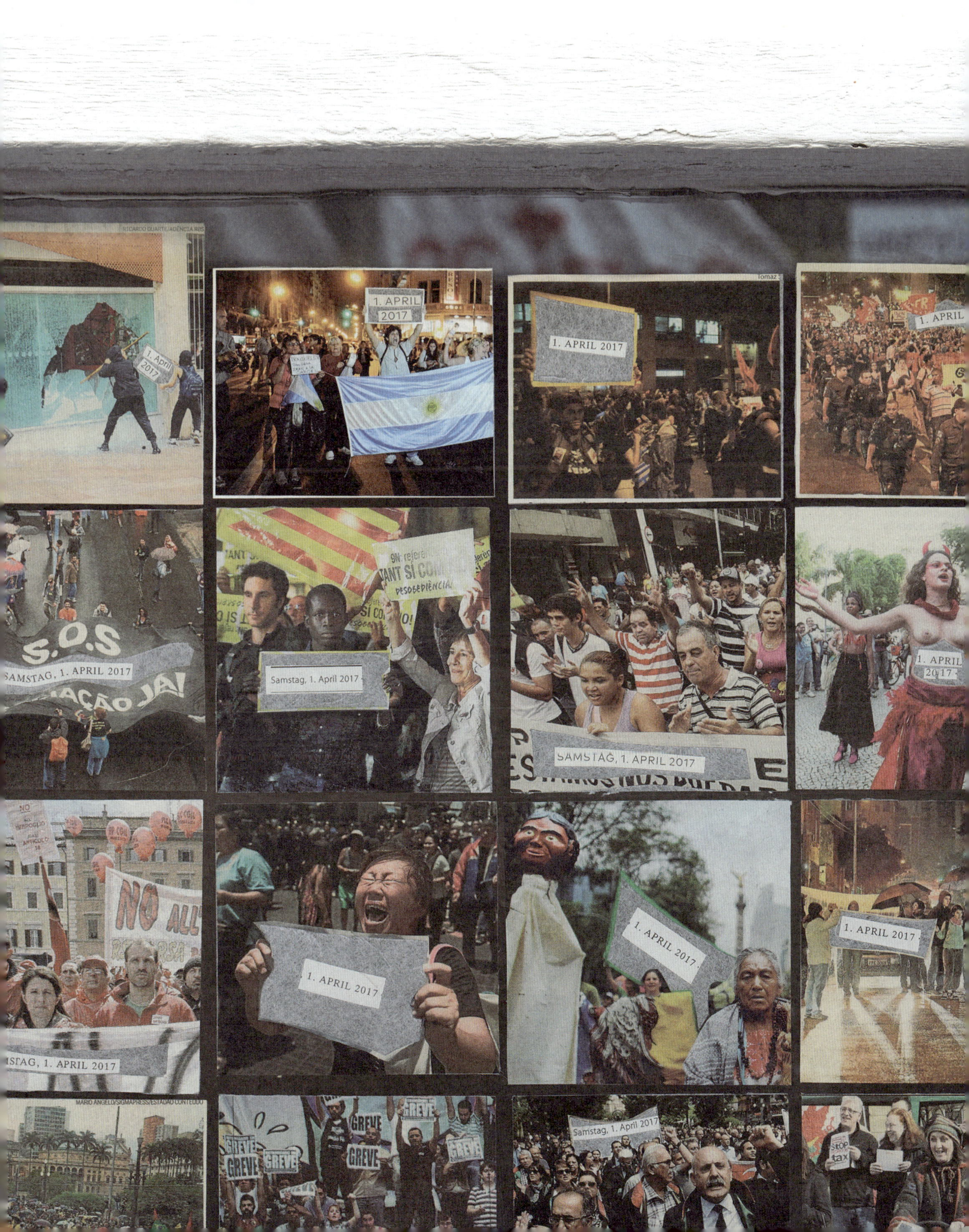
1. April 2017
1. APRIL 2017
1. APRIL 2017
1. APRIL
S.O.S
SAMSTAG, 1. APRIL 2017
Samstag, 1. April 2017
SAMSTAG, 1. APRIL 2017
1. APRIL 2017
SAMSTAG, 1. APRIL 2017
NO ALL'
1. APRIL 2017
1. APRIL 2017
1. APRIL 2017
GREVE
Samstag, 1. April 2017
STOP tax

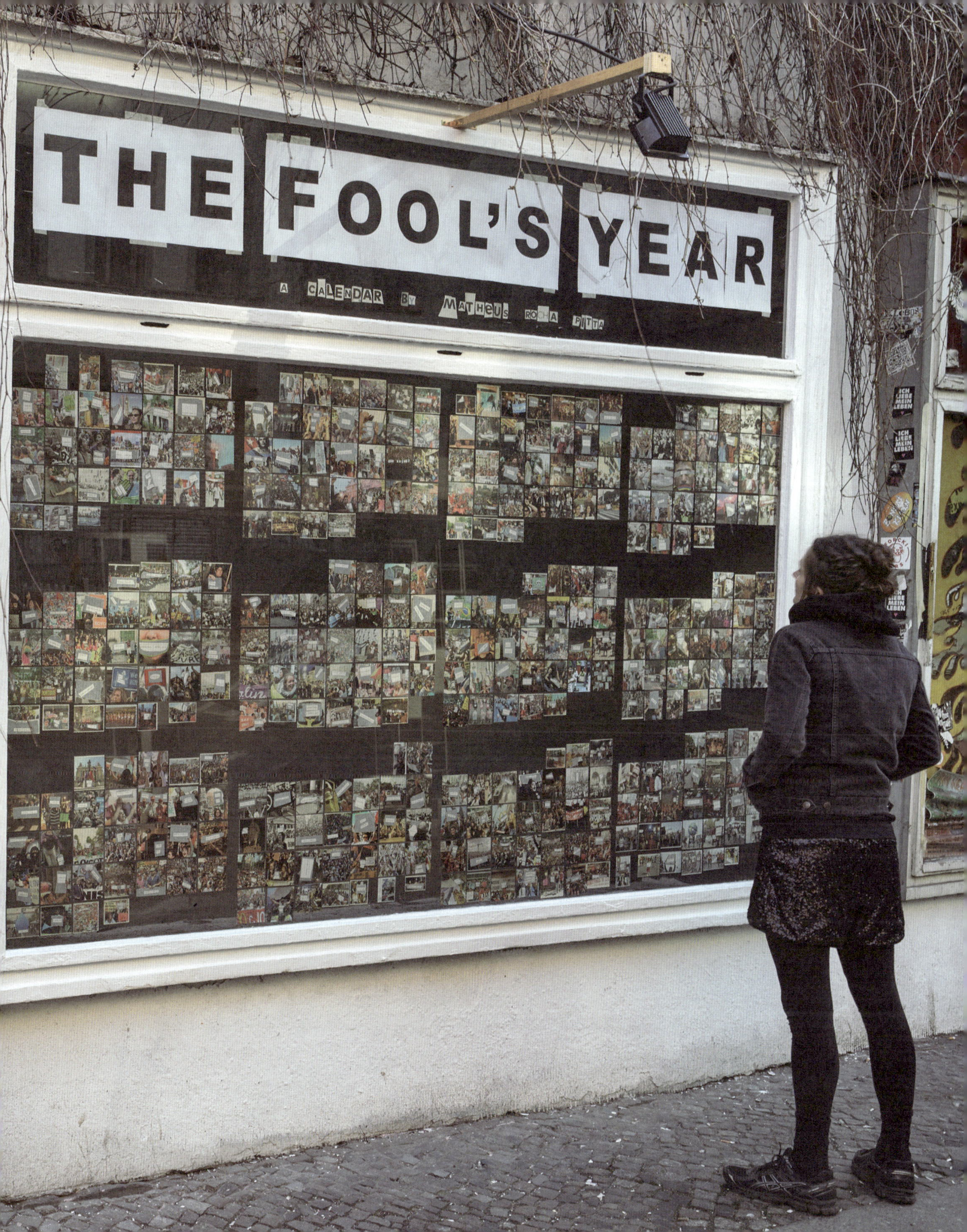
THE FOOL'S YEAR
A CALENDAR BY MATHEUS ROCHA PITTA

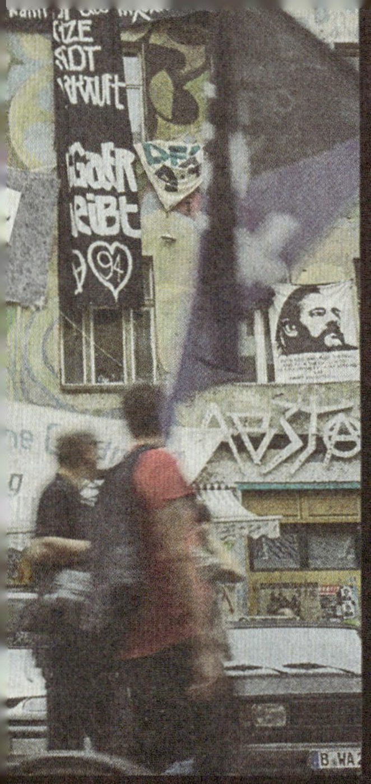

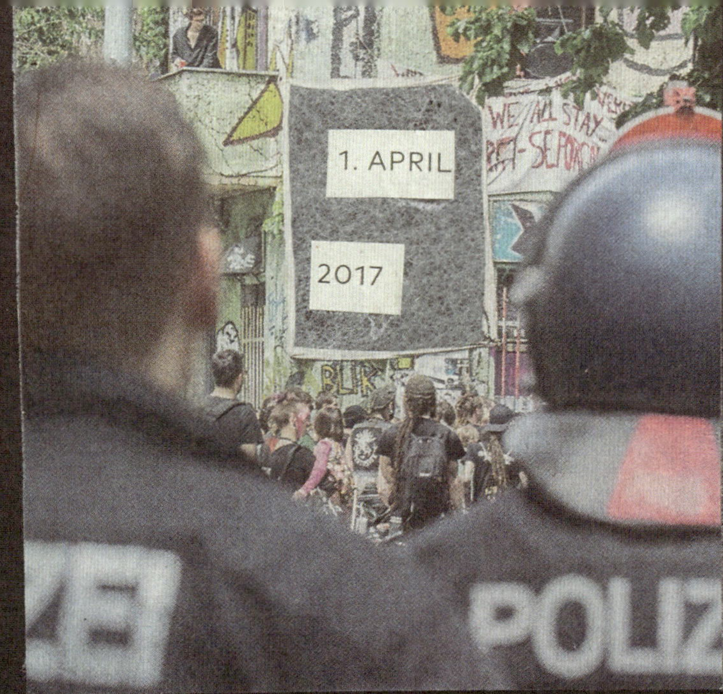
1. APRIL
2017
POLIZ

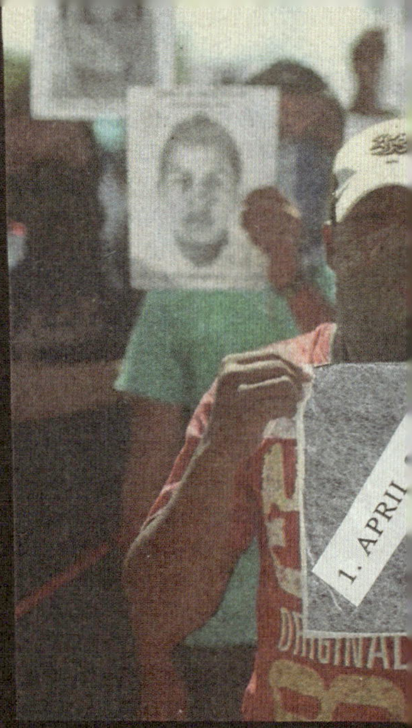
1. APRIL

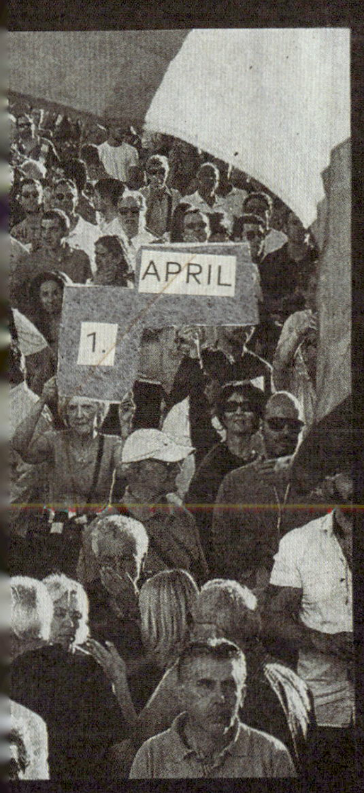
APRIL
1.

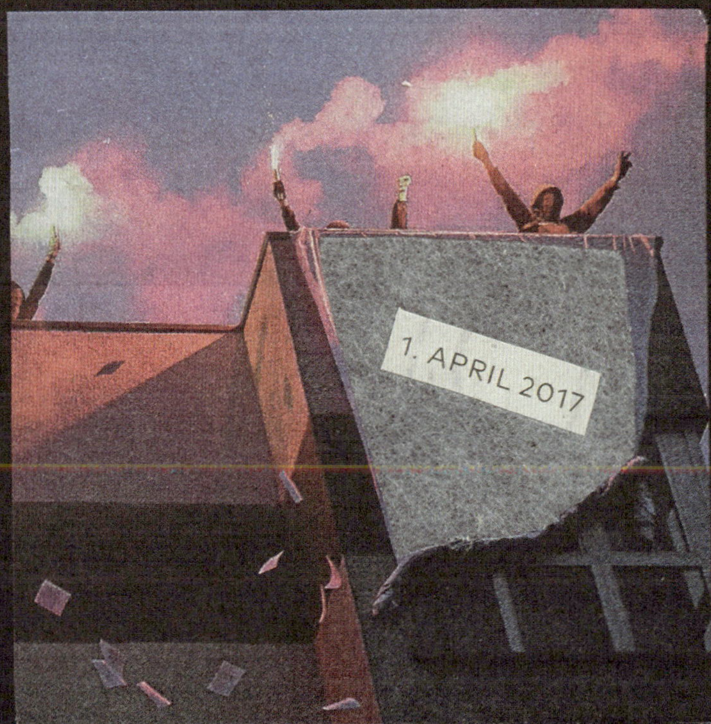
1. APRIL 2017

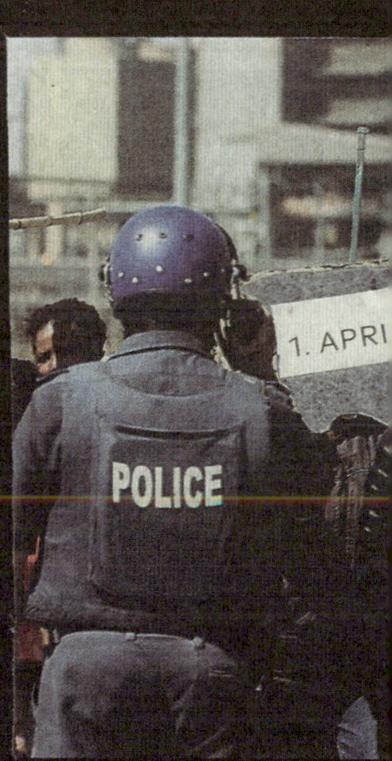
1. APRI
POLICE

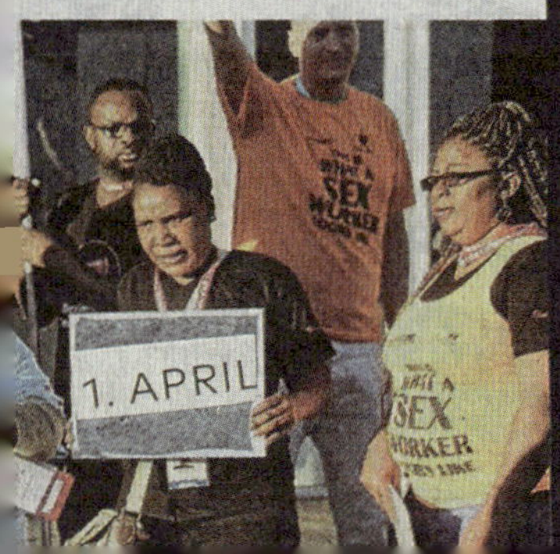
1. APRIL

About the artist:

Matheus Rocha Pitta (born 1980 in Tiradentes, MG, Brazil) has spent much time over the past years investigating forms and perceptions of gestures. Focusing on the intersection in everyday life and art, he disconnects gestures from their individual biographical background and portrays them as deliberate aesthetic acts with a historical dimension. Rocha Pitta uses photography, video and sculpture to identify and construct his own repertoire of gestures, which he activates in conjunction with the visitors and spectators of his works. He has created several series of works – *Primeira Pedra (The First Stone*, 2015*)*, *no hay pan (There Is No Bread*, 2015*)*, *Assalto (Assault*, 2014*)*, *Golpe de graça (Blow of Grace*, 2013*)* – that display gestures to explore language, possession and motion in a way that has far-reaching ethical implications.

About the author:

Tobias Peper studied Art History, Sociology and German Philology in Cologne. He is currently the curatorial assistant at the Kunstverein in Hamburg. Before, he was a trainee at the Migros Museum for Contemporary Art in Zurich and worked at the Museum Ludwig in Cologne. In 2012 and 2014, he was among others responsible for the art education at new talents – biennale cologne. He publishes regularly on the art of the 20th and 21st century, in recent years for example about Katja Novitskova, MOON & JEON and Xanti Schawinsky.

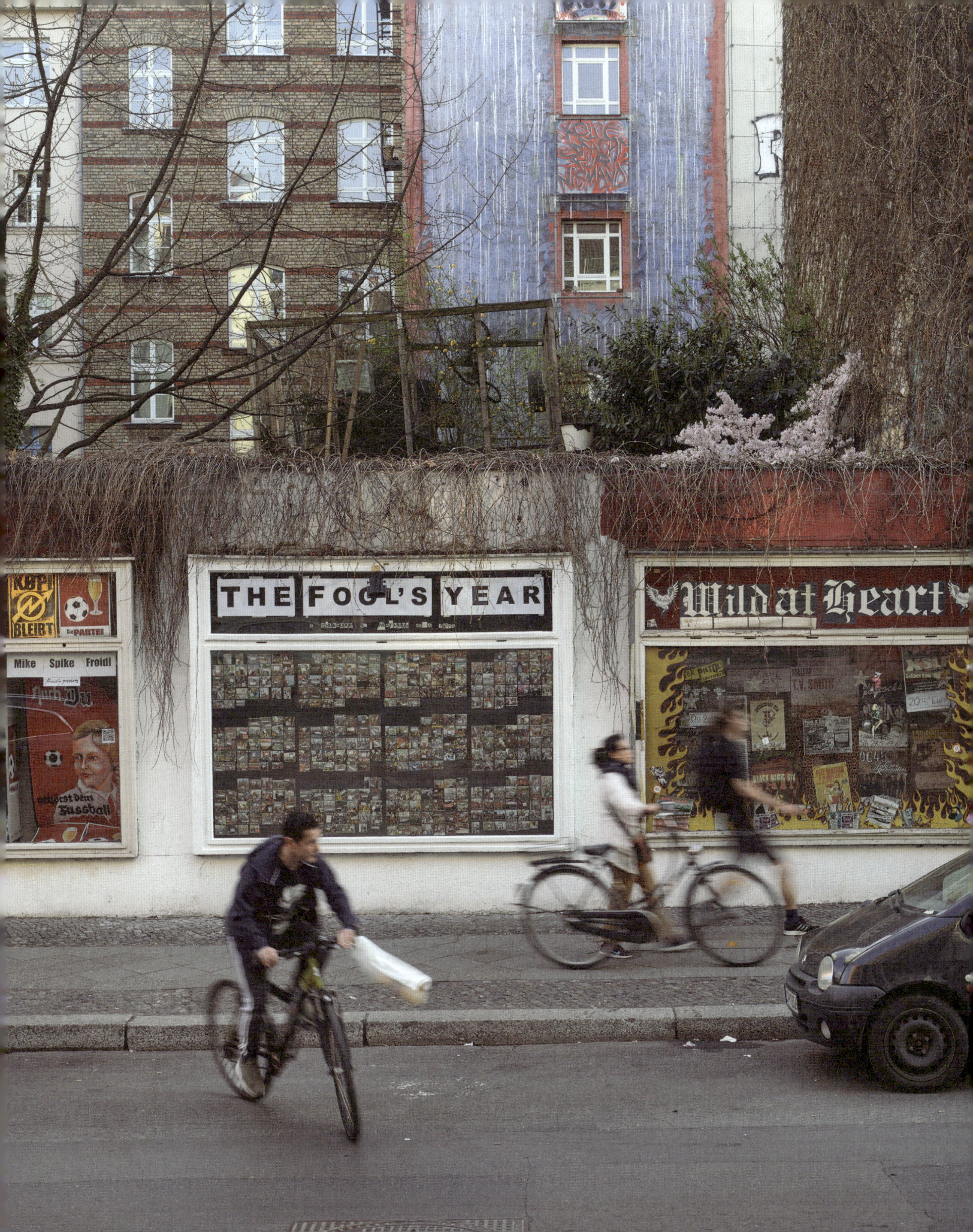
THE FOOL'S YEAR
Wild at Heart
Mike Spike Froidl

Matheus Rocha Pitta –
Aos Vencedores as Batatas
With an essay by Tobias Peper

Editors Herausgeber
Nicola Müllerschön
Christoph Tannert

Künstlerhaus Bethanien GmbH
Kohlfurter Str. 41/43
Showroom/Schauraum:
Kottbusser Str. 10
D-10999 Berlin
www.bethanien.de

Artistic Director
Künstlerische Leitung
Christoph Tannert

Administrative Director
Kaufmännische Leitung
Andrea Boche

International Studio Programme
Internationales Atelierprogramm
Valeria Schulte-Fischedick

Press & PR Presse
Christina Sickert

Administration Verwaltung
Ute Werner

Technical Staff Technik
Toni Lebkücher, Peter Rosemann

KfW Stiftung
Palmengartenstraße 5–9
D-60325 Frankfurt am Main
www.kfw-stiftung.de

Executive Director
Geschäftsführer
Bernd Siegfried

Programme Manager
Arts and Culture
Programmleiterin Kunst und Kultur
Nicola Müllerschön

Editing Redaktion
Christoph Tannert
Valeria Schulte-Fischedick
Malina Lauterbach

Copy-editing and Translation
Übersetzung
Aymone Rassaerts

Project Management/Design
Thorsten Probst/angenehme-gestaltung

Photos
Matheus Rocha Pitta (cover, pp. 1–49)
Eric Tschernow (pp. 51–63)

Production Gesamtherstellung
Druckerei Kettler GmbH, Bönen

Published by Erschienen bei
Verlag Kettler, Dortmund
www.verlag-kettler.de

This catalogue is published on the occasion of the exhibition *Aos Vencedores as Batatas* by Matheus Rocha Pitta, International Studio Programme, Künstlerhaus Bethanien, Berlin, March 3 to 26, 2017. Matheus Rocha Pitta is a grantee of KfW Stiftung, Frankfurt am Main.

Der Katalog erscheint anlässlich der Ausstellung *Aos Vencedores as Batatas* von Matheus Rocha Pitta im Rahmen des Internationalen Atelierprogramms des Künstlerhauses Bethanien, Berlin, vom 3. bis 26. März 2017. Matheus Rocha Pitta ist Stipendiat der KfW Stiftung, Frankfurt am Main.

The artist would like to acknowledge:
Marcos Brias, Salwa Aleryani, Polys Peslikas, Sebastian Biskup, Haydar Köyel, Mario Nuciforo and the team of Gluck50, Scot Surdez, Claudio Oliveira, the amazing team of SOX Berlin and Felipe Masini.

ISBN 978-3-86206-660-5

KÜNSTLERHAUS BETHANIEN

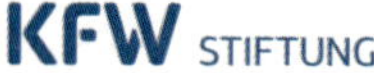